All in
on AI

Thomas H. Davenport Nitin Mittal

All in on AI

How Smart Companies Win Big with Artificial Intelligence

Harvard Business Review Press

Boston, Massachusetts

HBR Press Quantity Sales Discounts

Harvard Business Review Press titles are available at significant quantity discounts when purchased in bulk for client gifts, sales promotions, and premiums. Special editions, including books with corporate logos, customized covers, and letters from the company or CEO printed in the front matter, as well as excerpts of existing books, can also be created in large quantities for special needs.

For details and discount information for both print and ebook formats, contact booksales@harvardbusiness.org, tel. 800-988-0886, or www.hbr.org/bulksales.

Copyright 2023 Deloitte Development LLC

All rights reserved

Printed in the United States of America

10 9 8 7 6 5 4 3 2 1

No part of this publication may be reproduced, stored in or introduced into a retrieval system, or transmitted, in any form, or by any means (electronic, mechanical, photocopying, recording, or otherwise), without the prior permission of the publisher. Requests for permission should be directed to permissions@harvardbusiness.org, or mailed to Permissions, Harvard Business School Publishing, 60 Harvard Way, Boston, Massachusetts 02163.

The web addresses referenced in this book were live and correct at the time of the book's publication but may be subject to change.

Cataloging-in-Publication data is forthcoming.

ISBN: 978-1-64782-469-3
eISBN: 978-1-64782-470-9

The paper used in this publication meets the requirements of the American National Standard for Permanence of Paper for Publications and Documents in Libraries and Archives Z39.48-1992.

CONTENTS

All in on AI

INTRODUCTION

No one was terribly surprised when Sundar Pichai, the CEO of Alphabet (parent company of Google), announced at a 2017 Google customer event that the company would be moving to "AI first." In an address to technology developers, Pichai said, "In an AI-first world, we are rethinking all our products and applying machine learning and AI to solve user problems."[1] Even before that, in 2015, Google had tallied up more than 2,700 AI and machine-learning projects across the company.[2] AI is embedded in virtually all its products and services for customers, including search, maps, Gmail, Duo/Assistant, and many others. It offers TensorFlow, a set of machine-learning algorithms and tools, to Google Cloud customers. Several of Alphabet's other businesses, including its autonomous vehicle company Waymo and its biotech company Calico, also make extensive use of AI.

That Alphabet/Google was all-in on AI was well known at the time by industry observers, so the announcement didn't get a lot of attention. It was normal behavior for Silicon Valley and hard-charging digital native organizations. There is even a book about AI-first companies among tech startups, also perhaps to no one's surprise.[3] People seemed to think, "That's just what Google does—and for that matter Facebook, Amazon, Tencent, Alibaba, etc."

But Alphabet/Google and other tech organizations weren't the only ones thinking about powering their business with AI. There are legacy businesses and even small- to midsize companies that have

pursued the objective as well. For example, although few small businesses had AI on their radar screens at the time, radius financial
group, a 200-employee mortgage originator in the suburbs south of
Boston, did.[4] Keith Polaski, the cofounder of the company and head
of operations, began an intensive search for AI tools in 2016. Polaski
refers to his business as "loan manufacturing," and he measures
everything that happens in his mortgage manufacturing plant. He
put AI and automation tools to work, and now his company is substantially more productive and profitable than the average for the
industry.[5]

AI was supposedly taking place primarily in Silicon Valley, but
the European aviation giant Airbus didn't get the message. Realizing that it needed to adapt and improve operational efficiency in the
face of an aviation industry heavily disrupted by digitization, Airbus embarked in the mid-2010s on a broad digital transformation.
AI and data were front and center of the change, with a wide variety of initiatives across the company. It invested in new technology
and even began to retrain employees to use AI. Its program is no
secret: Airbus's website reports, "Artificial intelligence (AI) is much
more than a research field: it is a ubiquitous future technology with
the potential to redefine all areas of our society. At Airbus, we believe
AI is a key competitive advantage that enables us to capitalize on
the value of our data."[6]

Airbus applies its AI capabilities across the width and breadth of
its global organization, for its commercial airplane business as well
as its Helicopters, Defense, and Space divisions. AI technology has
been foundational for many Airbus offerings, including its OneAtlas
imagery service, ATTOL (vision-based navigation for autonomous
taxi, takeoff, and landing) demonstrator, vision-based navigation for
helicopters, and virtual assistants to pilots in cockpits and astro-
nauts in the International Space Station.

AI is certainly being aggressively pursued in China by digital
native organizations like Alibaba and Tencent. However, it's also

being applied to traditional businesses like insurance, banking, health care, and car sales. One giant company, Ping An, has thriving businesses in all those areas. It has used AI in each of them to rapidly pay insurance claims based on photos, determine identity using facial recognition for credit checks, enable intelligent telemedicine, and determine the value of used cars. Its business model is to offer lifestyle financial consumer products to customers and internet users in "ecosystems" covering financial services, automobile services, health care, and smart cities services, learning all the time from their data to refine their AI scenario models.

Something is working at Ping An; the company was only founded in 1988, and its 2020 revenues were nearly $200 billion. Again, it's not trying to hide its focus on AI; the website of Ping An Technology—the technology arm of Ping An—discloses: "Artificial intelligence is one of the core technologies of Ping An Technology, and has formed a series of solutions including predictive AI, cognitive AI and decision-making AI."[7] It further elaborates: "Ping An Technology has formed an intelligent cognition technology matrix, including facial recognition, voiceprint recognition, medical image AI reading, animal recognition and multimodal biometrics, which has gradually been widely and deeply used in real life." Even many tech firms couldn't put that statement on their websites.

Ping An, Airbus, and radius are traditional businesses. They are not tech or e-commerce companies, although they have substantial technology capabilities. They are typical of our focus on the role of AI in "legacy" companies. These are companies that take extensive advantage of the power of AI, even though it's not their core product or service offering. One head of AI at a retailer told us, "People ask me why I only take these data, analytics, and AI roles in legacy companies. It's because the job is too easy in born-digital businesses!" Although we suspect it's not as easy as it looks, we tend to agree. It is a hard thing to take an existing business in a traditional industry and go all-in on AI to transform its capabilities. As we did with

Google at the beginning of this section, we will occasionally refer to AI-intensive tech companies and startups when there is a lesson to be learned from them or when they are partnering with traditional businesses. But our primary examples will be in industries and even companies that existed before we were born. We'll describe banks, insurance companies, manufacturers, retailers and consumer products companies, information providers, life sciences companies, and even some government organizations. They have different business issues and customer needs, but they've all found their way to being all-in on AI.

Our focus in this book is on how large firms that existed well before AI are transforming themselves with the help of that technology. Instead of describing the average or most common approach to implementing AI, we'll profile the companies that are all-in on AI— they are making big and intelligent bets that this technology will lead to major business improvements, and they already have evidence that these bets are paying off. We refer to these companies' all-in approaches in multiple ways—"AI fueled," "AI powered," "AI enabled," etc. The common thread is that they are at the far end of the scale in their spending, planning, strategizing, implementing, and changing with regard to AI technology. Not every company will choose this ambitious approach, but we think that everyone can learn from it and perhaps even be inspired by it.

Our goal in the rest of these pages is to explore the concept of being all-in on AI and what is required for an organization to get there. Our perspective is a view of AI at its most extreme—the most aggressive adoption, the best integration with strategy and operations, the highest business value, the best implementation. We will describe the implications of aggressive AI usage for strategy, processes, technology, culture, and talent. Knowing what the leading adopters of AI are doing can be helpful to many other organizations as they attempt to assess the potential of the technology to transform their own business.

Our Experience

Both of us have had some experience working with and profiling such leading firms. Tom researched and wrote in the area of analytics for many years before moving into AI, and he wrote bestselling articles and books about "competing on analytics."[8] The HBR article by that name was even designated one of the twelve must-read articles in the magazine's 100-year history. The response to the articles and books made it clear that companies and their management could benefit from this all-in perspective even when they chose a more incremental approach. Since then Tom has worked with hundreds of companies around the world who wanted to build their analytical capabilities and then start to employ their close cousin, AI. Some of the companies he profiled in his writing on analytics, like Capital One and Progressive Insurance, also make an appearance in this book. However, they have undertaken multiple specific initiatives to increase their AI capabilities as well.

Nitin has been thinking about, speaking on, and working with clients on what it means to be AI fueled for several years now. He has also found that many executives who are only moderately knowledgeable about AI find it useful to know how companies are transforming themselves by leveraging the breadth of AI technologies. Prior to focusing on AI, he worked with health-care and life sciences companies for about fifteen years to help them embrace data and analytics in their businesses. And as the head of analytics and AI at Deloitte in the United States for over five years, he's been able to engage with clients and executives who themselves have transformational objectives for AI, as well as vendor partners who make and market some of the world's most sophisticated AI technologies.[9] Further, he leads a strategic initiative at Deloitte in the United States aimed at using AI to transform the world's largest professional services firm.

We both find AI fascinating, but even more interesting is the complex interplay of AI with business strategy and business models, key processes, organization and change management, and the existing technology architectures that established companies all have. Developing a great new algorithm is an impressive achievement, but no more so than pulling off a major business change initiative that includes AI. We like working with and writing about organizations that use technologies—AI in particular—to discover new ways of competing and doing business. That's the kind of story you'll find in this book.

What You'll Learn in This Book

As with the foregoing examples, we'll provide many descriptions of what AI-fueled companies are doing with AI. But they are contained within broader discussions of what it takes to be successful with AI at the "all-in" level. The chapter topics, and the companies featured in each chapter, include:

Chapter 1: What Does It Mean to Be AI Fueled?

We describe what it takes to be an AI-fueled organization, including the specific technologies that companies use, the ways they achieve value, and the components that define an all-in approach to AI. We mention a variety of companies in the chapter, but Ping An and DBS's digibank chatbot in India are singled out in some detail.

Chapter 2: The Human Side

We argue in this chapter that the most important attribute in AI success is not machinery, but human leadership, behavior, and change. We begin the chapter with a discussion of Piyush Gupta, the CEO of

DBS Bank, as an effective leader of his organization's AI initiative. We also discuss leadership issues at Morgan Stanley, Loblaw, and CCC Intelligent Solutions. In the area of improving the understanding and adoption of AI by both management and employees, we discuss Shell, Deloitte, Airbus, Bank of Montreal, Eli Lilly, and Unilever.

Chapter 3: Strategy

AI is capable of enabling or transforming business strategy, and how it does so is the focus of chapter 3. In it we describe three major strategic archetypes that AI organizations can adopt. In the course of describing these archetypes, we describe a variety of companies: Loblaw, Toyota, Morgan Stanley, Ping An, Airbus, Shell, SOMPO, Anthem, FICO, Manulife, Progressive, and Well.

Chapter 4: Technology and Data

You can't do advanced AI without some advanced technology and considerable data, so in chapter 4 we describe the components of a modern AI-oriented tech infrastructure and data environment. We discuss using all the tools in the AI toolbox, data for AI, automated machine learning or AutoML, machine learning operations or MLOps, legacy technologies, and scaling AI applications. Among the companies discussed in this chapter are DBS, the Kroger Co. (and its 84.51° subsidiary), Shell, Unilever, Anthem, and Airbus.

Chapter 5: Capabilities

AI, like any other business capability, can be assessed and ranked in terms of how far along a company is on various dimensions. Since there are different strategic archetypes for the use of AI, there are different capability models for each one. We describe the capabilities of Ping An in detail in this chapter, as well as Scotiabank, Manulife, Progressive, and Anthem. We also describe ethical AI capabilities in this chapter and focus on Unilever as our primary example.

Chapter 6: Industry Use Cases

Use cases or AI applications are at the core of how an organization applies the technology to its business issues. In this chapter we describe use cases across a variety of industries. We separate the list into common and less common use cases and provide examples of early and aggressive adopters in each industry. Companies featured include Walmart, Seagate, Capital One, the US and Singapore governments, Cleveland Clinic, Pfizer, Novartis, AstraZeneca, Eli Lilly, and Disney.

Chapter 7: Becoming AI Fueled

In the final chapter we describe a set of four alternative paths to becoming AI fueled. Each path is illustrated with a particular example. Deloitte is the example for the first path, which describes a move from being solely people-focused to people- and AI-focused in professional services. CCC Intelligent Solutions is the example for a path moving from a focus on information to a focus on AI. Capital One illustrates the path from an analytically focused company to an AI-focused one. Finally, Well—a health-care startup—is the illustration for starting from scratch to build a set of AI capabilities.

Despite all this content, the book is not a standard recipe for going all-in on AI. Every organization will vary in its rationale, strategy, and specific path for aggressively integrating AI into its business. We're confident, however, that the examples and lessons in this book will aid each organization in its individual journey. At a minimum, we hope that reading about what these early and leading organizations are doing with AI will provoke you to say about your own company, "We'd better get moving."

CHAPTER 1

What Does It Mean to Be AI Fueled?

Some—but not nearly enough—of the most successful and most technological organizations in the world have declared their intention to be all-in on artificial intelligence, or "AI first" or "AI fueled." Google described it as "a world that is AI-first, where computing becomes universally available—be it at home, at work, in the car, or on the go—and interacting with all of these surfaces becomes much more natural and intuitive, and above all, more intelligent."[1] Companies seeking to be powered by AI in other industries share the goal of intuitive technology and pervasive intelligence but are applying those objectives to their own industries, such as financial services, manufacturing, or health care.

The AI-fueled organizations in our analysis comprise less than 1 percent of large companies. It wasn't easy to find enough to write about in this book, but we were able to discover about thirty. We expect, however, that many more organizations will move in this direction. And why wouldn't they? The companies we describe in this book perform well. They have effective business models, make good decisions, have close relationships with customers, offer desirable products and services, and charge profitable prices. They have become learning machines, and their people are accelerated by AI. They are typically able to do these things because they have more and better data than other companies that is analyzed and acted upon by AI, and they use these resources to build their businesses and create economic and social value.

For many organizations, harnessing artificial intelligence's full potential begins tentatively with explorations of select enterprise opportunities and a few potential use cases. Many never get to the only step that can add economic value—deploying a model into production. While testing the waters this way may deliver valuable insights, it likely won't be enough to make a company a market maker, or even a fast follower. To achieve substantial value from AI, a company should fundamentally rethink the way humans and machines interact within working environments. It needs to make very large investments in AI. It should work not only on AI pilots, but on full production deployments that change how employees work and how customers interface with the company. Executives should consider deploying AI tools systematically across every key function and enterprise operation to support new business process designs and data-driven decision-making. Likewise, AI should drive new product and service offerings and business models. For the moment, using AI in this aggressive fashion confers industry leadership. Eventually, becoming an AI-fueled organization is likely to be more than a strategy for business success—it could be table stakes for survival.

What Are the Components of AI Fuel?

How do you know that an organization is powered by AI? What components does it need to assemble in order to deserve that classification? There's no agreed-upon list, but in our research and consulting, we've seen a variety of attributes that commonly turn up in the companies with a particularly aggressive approach to the technology. We've done three surveys of companies' AI activities over the past four years, so we can also attach some numbers to many of these, at least as of our last survey in October 2021.

Broad enterprise adoption of AI, using multiple technologies

Companies that are fueled by AI use it across their organizations, adopting multiple use cases or applications. AI is a general-purpose technology, and it can be used to support a wide variety of business goals and objectives. According to our surveys, AI technologies are most commonly applied in making business processes more efficient, improving decisions, and enhancing existing products and services. These are also the three most likely objectives to have already been achieved, according to the 2020 Deloitte survey, when the question was last asked.[2] But those cover a wide variety of usage domains for AI. Business process improvements, for example, might include better matching supply and demand for supply chain effectiveness, predicting the need for maintenance in factory equipment, or even predicting which employee candidates will work out best if hired. All-in-on-AI companies eventually develop use cases across a wide variety of functions and processes, decisions, and products or services. Each individual application may not transform the company, but the broad collection of them can.

In our most recent enterprise AI survey, the companies with the most AI capabilities and achievements—labeled "transformers"—comprised 28 percent of the survey sample. As we'll describe below, transformers are well along in their AI journeys, but very few of the respondents in this category are yet AI fueled (those companies number too few to be picked up in a broad survey). On average, the group had about six full-scale deployments of AI-use cases, and about seven business outcomes achieved—impressive, but short of what an AI-fueled company would have. The label "transformers" suggests that their goal may be business transformation, but very few have yet been transformed by AI. Companies relying on AI to transform themselves typically go much further in this regard; some have hundreds of deployed systems and business outcomes too numerous to count. Of course, business transformation is a continuous process, and no company is ever fully transformed.

Companies that are all-in on AI also don't restrict their AI portfolios to a single technology. Instead, they take advantage of all that AI has to offer. The many technologies that make up the field are described in table 1-1. Only four basic resources make AI possible—knowledge in the forms of statistics, logic, and semantics, all strung together with computation—but within those families there are multiple variations of methods, tools, and use cases.

Leaders of AI-fueled enterprises learn enough about the technology to make smart decisions about which technologies go into which use cases. It's not always easy to do so; there are some complexities hidden among the different tools. For example, table 1-1 lists several different types of machine learning, and aggressive users of the technology need to know which to adopt for what purpose. In addition, there are choices within choices to be made. For example, "semantics-based AI" in table 1-1 describes language-oriented applications, such as natural language understanding (NLU) and natural language generation (NLG). But NLU applications can have deep-learning algorithms at their core, as well as knowledge graphs illustrating the connections among words and concepts suggested by the term "semantics." And NLG applications can as well, as in the very sophisticated GPT-3 system developed by OpenAI that can generate all sorts of text types based on next-word predictions, from poems to computer programs. Simple NLG applications can also be driven by rules. The complexities of describing AI technology types suggest that executives making decisions about AI need to do their homework before making major investments in tools and projects.

TABLE 1-1

AI technologies employed by AI-fueled companies

Type of AI technology	How it works
Statistical machine learning	
Supervised machine learning	Creates prediction models trained on past data
Unsupervised machine learning	Identifies groupings of similar cases, with no training
Self-supervised learning	Finds supervisory signals in data. An emerging approach
Reinforcement learning	Learns by experimentation and maximizing a reward
Neural networks	Uses hidden layers of features to predict/classify
Deep learning	Uses many hidden layers for predictive models
Deep learning image recognition	Learns to recognize images from labeled datasets
Deep learning natural language processing	Learns to understand or generate speech and text
Logic-based AI systems	
Rule engines	Makes simple decisions based on if/then rules
Robotic process automation	Combines workflow, data access, and rule-based decisions
Semantics-based AI	
Speech recognition	Recognizes human speech and converts it to text
Natural language understanding	Assesses textual content for meaning and intent
Natural language generation	Creates customized, readable text

Some companies use multiple technologies for the same use case or application. Cotiviti, an insurance fraud detection and health-care analytics company, uses rules in combination with machine learning, which is a useful pairing. DBS Bank uses the same combination to fight money laundering. Many companies are using robotic process automation (RPA), which automates back-office structured workflows and makes decisions with rules. But increasing numbers of vendors and their customers are combining RPA with machine learning for better decision-making; this is sometimes called "intelligent process automation." More and more we will see these technologies combined and perhaps given new names. Aggressive adopters are likely to adopt all the AI technologies—some as described in table 1-1, and some in combined forms that we can't fully describe today but that are just beginning to emerge. Virtual reality and other forms of simulations, digital twins, and metaverses are all technologies that employ various forms of AI and are likely to be widely adopted in the future.

Many AI systems in production deployment

One of the challenges of AI is getting systems into production deployment. Many companies embark on pilots, proofs of concept, or prototypes, but they put few or none of them into production. It's great to learn from such experiments, but companies don't get any economic value from them. AI-fueled organizations do manage to get systems into production; the most recent survey of enterprise AI found that the transformers, the most successful and experienced companies responding to the survey, had on average six production deployments of AI. That put them in the most aggressive survey category, but some of the companies we interviewed for this book had many more AI models in production.[3]

Despite the relative success of AI-powered enterprises, there is much other survey data to support our assertion that deployment is difficult. A 2021 IBM survey found that of over five thousand technology decision-makers in seven countries, only 31 percent said their company had "actively deployed AI as part of its business operations." Forty-one percent of the surveyed companies said they were "exploring, but have not deployed, AI in business operations."[4] In a 2019 MIT Sloan Management Review/Boston Consulting Group survey, "seven out of 10 companies surveyed report minimal or no impact from AI so far. Among the 90% of companies that have made some investment in AI, fewer than 2 out of 5 report business gains from AI in the past three years. . . . this means 40% of organizations making significant investments in AI do not report business gains from

AI."[5] In our survey, the top three challenges with AI were implementation issues, integrating AI into the company's roles and functions, and data issues—all factors involved in large-scale deployment.[6] This situation is starting to change, and companies are beginning to report that they are deploying more AI systems and getting more economic returns from them.[7] Surveys of data scientists, however, still find that a minority of AI models are actually deployed.

It's not surprising that companies would face challenges with deployment. Pilots involve creating a model and coding up a minimum viable product. But production deployments require much greater scale, and usually involve many other activities, like changing business processes, upskilling workers, and integrating with existing systems. In addition, some data scientists think their job ends at creating a good machine learning model that fits the data. Deployment is often considered someone else's job—though it's often not clear whose.

How do highly successful AI-user companies address these issues and get systems deployed? First, they plan on deployment from the beginning unless there is a problem in the early phases of a project. Second, they often put someone in charge of the entire process of development and deployment—sometimes referred to as a *product manager* for AI-based systems and processes—who ensures that the system is deployed. Third, they assign data scientists and product managers who work closely with stakeholders on the business side from the beginning. These companies expect deployment and all the activities associated with it to take place.

Employing AI to reimagine and reengineer work processes

In the early 1990s, many businesspeople got excited about something called *business process reengineering*, a movement in which companies engaged in radical redesign of how they did their work (one of us—Tom—helped to create this movement). There were new technologies then—enterprise resource planning (ERP) systems, and eventually the internet—that could enable new process flows. Unfortunately, reengineering devolved into mindless headcount reductions at many organizations, but the idea of using new technology—and AI is now the most prominent example—to drive new ways of working is still a valid one.

Deloitte has referred to the current era as the "Age of With"—meaning that people are working collaboratively with smart machines. And Tom has liked that idea—which he often refers to as "augmentation"—enough to have coauthored two books on the subject.[8] While many prognosticators have predicted that AI would replace humans, not much of that has taken place thus far, and most organizations are using the technology to free up human workers to do more complex tasks. The primary issue facing AI-powered companies, then, is not how to replace human workers with AI, but how to get the best out of both by redesigning jobs, reskilling workers, and becoming more efficient and effective in the process.

In our surveys, high percentages of executives already say that AI has led to moderate or substantial changes in jobs (72 percent in the survey from 2019, with 82 percent expecting that much change in three years). In many cases, however, that change isn't done in a formal business process context. That means it may lack a description of process workflows, measurement, and consistent implementation across an organization.

The closest connection between process improvement—if not radical innovation—and AI is probably with RPA. Some don't view RPA as having enough intelligence to be called AI, but it does have rule-based decision capabilities. Many companies view RPA as a stepping-stone to more intelligent and machine learning–based AI. Several companies have integrated RPA into their process improvement programs. Before they automate a process, they apply measurement and improvement techniques to it. At the retirement and financial services firm Voya, for example, an automation center of excellence is embedded within the company's Continuous Improvement Center, which generally uses Lean and Six Sigma methods. Voya has a three-step procedure for analyzing and improving a process, implementing RPA for it, and then assessing the performance of the automated process.[9] In order to be truly transformed by AI, however, a company would have to do this on a broad scale and at least occasionally seek more than incremental performance improvements in a process.

We have seen a few companies that have effectively combined process reengineering and forms of AI other than RPA. DBS Bank in Southeast Asia, for example, used AI to enable major process improvements in its anti–money laundering (AML) efforts, as well as in its customer centers in India and Singapore. It has reduced the time to evaluate a potential AML case by a third. In the customer centers, it has grown the number of customers six times and financial transactions twelve times without adding staff.

More companies should address how AI can make possible dramatic improvements in business processes. To some degree this will be facilitated by a new technology that employs AI: *process mining.* It analyzes data from enterprise transactional systems to understand how the process is being performed, and then uses AI to make improvement recommendations. Process mining takes a lot of the detailed work out of process improvement and is catching on rapidly in many process-oriented companies.

A high percentage of the organization fluent in AI and how it can be applied

As we'll argue more than once in this book, being all-in on AI is as much about people as technology. Companies that want to use a lot of AI in their businesses need a lot of executives and employees who understand how it works. Smart companies are reskilling and upskilling their employees to develop, interpret, and improve

AI systems. This is becoming even more important as AI system development—particularly machine learning—becomes increasingly automated, and citizen data scientists without deep professional training can take over some of the load.

Executives need their own version of AI upskilling. Most heads of AI and analytics tell us that they still spend a lot of time evangelizing to other managers about the value and purpose of the technology. Executives not only should furnish the funding and time for AI projects but implement AI in their own work as well. AI can often automate decisions, and sometimes these are decisions previously made by human senior managers. So, it's important to educate this group on how AI works, when it's appropriate, and what a major commitment to it involves for themselves and the broader organization.

It's still early days for this upskilling and reskilling work for the great majority of companies, and not every employee needs to be trained in AI. But it's clear that some do, and probably the more the better. Some firms, like Airbus and DBS Bank, have embarked on upskilling programs that are specifically aimed at inculcating AI skills. Airbus has retrained more than a thousand employees in AI and advanced analytics skills. DBS Bank has trained over eighteen thousand employees in data skills, creating a company of citizen data scientists. About two thousand of these employees are proficient in advanced areas of data science and business intelligence, and another seven thousand have been identified to be upskilled in disciplines such as the use of data, analytics, and AI.

However, in one of our AI surveys, only 10 percent of US respondents stated a clear preference for retraining and keeping current employees. Eighty percent leaned toward either "keeping or replacing employees in equal measure" or "primarily replac[ing] current employees with new talent."[10] We believe this is shortsighted, and that companies won't be able to find or afford that much new AI talent. Retraining and upskilling is an obvious alternative approach.

Long-term commitments to and investment in AI

A decision by a company's senior executives to be transformed by AI is not a casual one. They are making a decision that will have a major influence on the company for decades and ultimately involve hundreds of millions or billions of dollars. Every company we interviewed for this book told us that's the cost of committing to be all-in on AI. At first such resource commitments may be scary for organizations, but after seeing the types of benefits they received from early projects, these AI-powered companies found it much easier to spend on AI-oriented data, technologies, and people.

Becoming AI focused is a commitment to use data and analytics for most decisions, to deal differently with customers, to embed AI into products and services, and to conduct many tasks and even entire business processes in a more automated and intelligent fashion. Lots of companies are in the throes of digital transformation, but an AI-based transformation goes much further. In short, it's a big bet, and most organizations don't yet have the intestinal fortitude to make it.

It helps, of course, if the leader is a strong advocate of the idea. CEO commitment drives a lot of other types of commitment in companies. But that's ultimately not enough. If upper, middle, and even frontline managers are only paying lip service to the idea of driving their business with AI, things will move slowly, and the organization will likely move back to its old habits. We've seen some highly committed CEOs build analytics and AI-focused companies with multiple initiatives. But then they left, and the next CEO wasn't a believer, so the focus on data, analytics, and AI lapsed into mediocrity.

We'll have more to say about the importance of leadership and commitment in the next chapter. And we'll describe some examples of leaders who exhibit commitment to AI as a strategic force in comprehensive and dramatic ways.

Unique and voluminous sources of data, analyzed and acted upon in real time

If AI can fuel a company, data fuels AI. Companies that are serious about AI must be serious about data—collecting it, integrating it, storing it, and making it broadly accessible. None of these is a new challenge, but it is even more important than normal if an organization cares about AI. In our 2020 AI survey, when asked to select the top initiative for increasing their competitive advantage from AI, companies that had adopted AI picked "modernizing our data infrastructure for AI" as their top choice. Virtually all the companies we spoke with had major data management projects underway before or at the same time as their AI initiatives.

In addition to having good data, companies who aspire to transform their businesses with AI must increasingly have some unique or proprietary data. If every competitor in an industry has the same data, they will all have similar machine learning models and similar outcomes from them. Part of differentiating your company with AI is finding an existing source of data that hasn't been fully exploited or getting access to new data types.

Banks and retail establishments are in industries where data is already voluminous. But banks like Scotiabank in Canada, Capital One in the United States, and DBS in Singapore use their data to learn more about customers and transactions and turn that data back to customers to help them manage their finances. Retail companies like the Kroger Co. in the United States and Loblaw in Canada simply make more use of point-of-sale data, inventory data, shopper loyalty data, and so forth—perhaps more than any of their competitors.

In some cases, companies that aggressively adopt AI have developed new business models that have allowed greater access to data. Ping An in China has a very conscious "ecosystem" model that gives it access not only to customers and suppliers, but also to data analytic models. Skywise, Airbus's open data platform for aviation, enables data sharing among many of the global airlines that fly Airbus aircraft and other original equipment manufacturers. These companies learned from e-commerce startups with platform business models that having data from multiple players is an important driver of growth and enterprise value.

Companies that rely heavily on AI don't just collect data and analyze it when they get around to it. They have a real-time approach whenever possible that allows data-based decisions to be made at the speed of contemporary business. They provide customer offers and prevent fraudulent transactions in real time at the point of sale. They react faster to business disruptions. They monitor how well their models are performing and retrain them if necessary. This is in part because of their modern technology stack, but also because they have processes in place to manage the data supply chain and a sense of urgency about harnessing data. Of course, no company's data is perfect, but AI-intensive companies have data environments that are far better than most.

A framework for ethical and trustworthy AI in place

If a company is relying heavily on AI in its business, it needs to ensure that the AI systems it uses are ethical and trustworthy, or it's likely to lose more from AI than it gains. Thus far, most of the formal governance mechanisms and structures for AI ethics are in tech organizations, which both have lots of AI products and services, and wish to demonstrate to customers that they are responsible. Perhaps because they were relatively early adopters of AI, tech companies have also been the most likely to have been accused of AI bias or other ethical infractions in the past.[11]

But it doesn't require a massive effort to create an approach to ethical and trustworthy AI. Many available frameworks can help create a set of principles; we discuss them in chapter 5. Of course, the challenge is putting principles into practice—which we also discuss in that chapter.

It would be possible to create a small group of executives with strong technical and business expertise to assess each of these criteria for each AI system to be put into production. Indeed, we have heard of several companies that have put groups like algorithm review boards in place, although we would suggest that more than the algorithm needs to be reviewed. One ethics consultant has called for an AI institutional review board, like those used for academic or medical research on human subjects, to ensure that no aspect of an AI system violates ethical principles.[12] After all, AI work also usually involves human subjects.

How Do AI-Fueled Companies Achieve Value?

The specific value levers that AI-fueled businesses use to create more value than many other companies are listed in figure 1-1. We will refer to these throughout the book. Suffice it to say here that AI-fueled companies often use multiple levers—sometimes in the same use case—to improve their businesses.

At the individual use case level, the DBS AML application that we mentioned earlier in this chapter has brought value to the bank in multiple ways. It allows DBS to identify fraud earlier, so it benefits speed to execution. Transaction surveillance analysts can analyze a potential AML case faster, and that increased productivity leads to cost reduction. It uses more of the bank's data—that is, comprehends complexity—to come to a decision about how likely a case is truly fraudulent. And of course, the overall purpose of the AML application is to fortify trust in the bank by its customers and regulators.

Of course, the more value achieved, the better. Companies that wish to succeed with AI should employ as many different value levers

---

FIGURE 1-1

How all-in-on-AI companies achieve value

Speed to execution: Apply AI to accelerate time to operational and business results by minimizing latency in decision-making and action.

Cost reduction: Apply AI to intelligently automate business processes, tasks, and interactions to reduce cost, increase efficiency, improve environmental sustainability, and ensure predictability.

Comprehension of complexity: Apply AI to improve understanding and decision-making by deciphering patterns, connecting dots, and predicting outcomes from increasingly complex data sources.

Transformed engagement: Apply AI to change how customers and employees interact with smart systems to expand means of engagement via voice, vision, text, and touch.

Fueled innovation: Apply AI to generate deep insights on where to play and how to win, enabling the creation of new products, market opportunities, and business models.

Fortified trust: Apply AI to secure one's brand from risks such as fraud, waste, abuse, and cyberintrusion, consequently assuring stakeholders and enhancing trust amongst customers.

---

as possible and strive to achieve multiple levers with individual use cases. Some of the levers, such as cost reduction, are relatively easy to measure. However, companies should not restrict themselves just to AI use cases that are easily measured. Some of the greatest benefits may arise from AI that changes the business model, makes decisions based on greater amounts and more complex types of data, and builds trust.

Where Are Companies on Their Journeys to All-In?

Having read about all the components of an AI-fueled company, you probably feel that your organization has some but not all of them, or that you're making progress toward these attributes but aren't fully there. The characterizations below may help you assess where you are. We will describe them further in chapter 5 when we discuss AI capabilities.

- *AI fueled.* Have all or most of the components we've described above, fully implemented and functioning—the business is built on AI capabilities and is becoming a learning machine (see the next section);

- *Transformers.* Are not yet AI fueled but are relatively far along in the journey, with some of the attributes in place; have multiple AI deployments that are creating substantial value for the organization;

- *Pathseekers.* Have already started on the journey and are making progress, but at an early stage—have some deployed systems and a few measurable positive outcomes achieved;

- *Starters.* Are experimenting with AI—they have a plan but need to do a lot more to progress; have very few or no production deployments in place;

- *Underachievers.* Have started experimenting with AI but have no production deployments and have achieved little to no economic value.

Not every company we mention in the book is AI fueled; in some cases, we describe organizations that are transformers or even pathseekers, but they have adopted useful or noteworthy practices.

Becoming an Organizational Learning Machine

One way of summarizing all these attributes is to think of all-in on AI companies as organizational learning machines. In such businesses, many aspects of AI-related learning are institutionalized and well oiled. They are organizational learning machines in at least two senses: First, they are continuously learning from their research and deployment of AI. They experiment and adopt rapid trial-and-error processes to extract lessons from what works and what doesn't. They have, as our colleagues John Hagel and John Seely Brown put it, achieved "scalable learning."[13] Both the experimentation and the learning are important to being world-class at AI.

For example, Ping An, the China-based company that began in insurance and now has moved into a variety of financial services-associated business areas (more about them in chapter 3), has a large research group and hires many talented PhDs in computer science and related fields. The company's founder, Peter Ma Mingzhe, is an art collector and suggested to the chief scientist, Jing Xiao, that an AI system that could create art and music might appeal to the company's extensive network of customers and partners. Xiao commissioned a small team to try to create paintings, musical compositions, and poetry by training a machine learning system on existing high-quality examples.

The experiment worked: the researchers were able to create high-quality art, music, and poems. The system was introduced at the 2019 World Artificial Intelligence Conference and received positive press mentions.[14] The music composition system even won an international award. Xiao told us in an interview that Ping An is working on business models that connect the arts AI system to different ecosystems of the group, such as using AI-created music for online medication or other health-care-related services. Meanwhile, his team learned about how to develop AI systems for businesses involving the subjective emotions or feelings of participants, such as trading in the securities market.

The other way in which AI-fueled companies become organizational learning machines relates directly to machine learning (at least the supervised form of it, which is by far the most common type in business). That technology makes predictions of unknown outcomes based on models trained on past data for which outcomes are known. It may sound a bit confusing, but companies that are organizational learning machines are constantly learning from their machine learning. What contemporary AI capability has essentially done is to make it possible and economical to productionize learning at scale and speed.

AI-fueled companies monitor their models to understand how successful their predictions are (often using a technology called *machine learning operations*). If the model stops making accurate predictions, the company uses new data to retrain the model and improve its predictions. In that way, the continuous training creates continuous learning and a more valuable model that fits the new data. In other words, if the world changes, the company's predictive models change with it.

A true learning machine company would do this for a whole variety of models, or at least the important ones. Doing so suggests that the company believes its models are valuable business assets worthy of monitoring and improving, recognizes that model accuracy can drift over time, and knows that technologies are available to facilitate the process of model operations. These capabilities are exactly the type that an AI-powered company would want to cultivate.

Of course, organizational learning machines can learn continuously from other types of AI as well. DBS Bank, for example, implemented chatbots—initially at its digital bank in India—as a means of providing high-quality customer service with no waiting and 24-7 availability to bank customers. During a review of a service failure in 2016, management challenged the team to monitor the customer journey more closely and detect issues before they happen.

The challenge inspired the team to come up with a new customer science program for digibank in India where they would monitor the journeys of every single digibank customer on a real-time basis. They would proactively look for indications of when the customer was struggling with using the mobile app, develop the ability to intervene when that was happening, and give the customer options for how to proceed with their journey. The learning was successful, and the chatbot learnings were applied both in India and in the home market of Singapore.

The final meaning of the term *organizational learning machine* focuses on the fact that these companies are consistent, reliable, and indefatigable. Their focus on AI in transforming their business is as relentless as any well-performing machine. They invest in AI infrastructure such as feature stores (repositories of well-defined variables for use in machine learning models) and algorithm libraries that can be reused many times across the organization. They ensure that many employees are also continuous learners about AI. They treat AI not as a fad but as a very powerful tool that can make them dramatically more efficient and effective in the marketplace.

Of course, it's not just technology that creates organizational learning machines. It's the combination of organizational DNA, a corporate culture that's supportive of AI and data-driven decisions, an attitude of continual experimentation and innovation, and engagement of employees, customers, and business partners in these pursuits. Human beings make these things happen, not data or algorithms or high-powered servers. Throughout this book we'll concentrate as much on the human dimension of being AI focused as on the technological capabilities. That's the focus of the next chapter.

As a concluding thought, it's great news that some organizations have all these capabilities. We consider it a privilege to speak with and to write about them. However, we wish there were more. Perhaps by describing the companies that stand out in this regard, we can motivate the readers of this book to move their own organizations in this direction—even though they may not achieve "all-in" status.

CHAPTER 2

The Human Side

A variety of factors affect an organization's AI capabilities and success that don't involve technology or even data. Leadership, culture, attitudes, and skills are human attributes that affect AI as much as or more than any other aspect of a company. If we were predicting whether a company would become AI powered using a machine learning model, these features would be highly influential in our model.

Many AI leaders acknowledge the importance of these factors. For example, we interviewed the leaders of a new research center at a biology-focused academic research institute—the Broad Institute in Cambridge, Massachusetts. The Institute received a $250 million grant to understand the connections between machine learning and biology. When we asked the codirectors of the new Eric and Wendy Schmidt Center at the Institute what issues might prevent them from achieving this goal, they both mentioned culture first. They said that AI people—typically computer scientists—and biologists have very different languages and intuitions for how to approach intellectual challenges. They knew that being able to connect these communities would be crucial to the success of the center.

When asked what they planned to do about these cultural issues, they were still at the stage of exploring potential strategies (it was early in the center's history). Foremost among them was hosting events that brought the two communities together to deeply discuss opportunities at the interface of the two fields and approaches to pursuing them. Certainly, they recognized that the science of change management for AI/biology collaboration is probably less advanced than the AI/biology collaboration itself.

Until we take active steps to manage these human issues, we are unlikely to make substantial progress on them. This is probably the reason why many companies—even large companies with enormous technology budgets—are not becoming more data-driven over time. Surveys of large US organizations have suggested that the percentage saying they have data-driven cultures has even declined in recent years.[1] We'll describe some of the interventions that AI-first companies have taken to address these issues later in this chapter.

A major factor in any organization's progress toward extensive use of AI is supportive, even enthusiastic leadership. We'll start this chapter with a description of one CEO who has played a very effective role in his company in inspiring and guiding its AI journey.

Portrait of an AI Leader

Piyush Gupta, the Group CEO of DBS Bank, has been in the conservative banking industry for almost forty years. Yet somehow he has managed to create not only a banking and customer service powerhouse out of the bank once known as Damn Bloody Slow, but has also become a highly aggressive adopter of artificial intelligence. His efforts are a powerful illustration of the impact of a senior executive leader on the effective adoption of a new technology.

Gupta arrived at DBS as CEO in 2009, when the company was ranked lowest in customer service among Singapore banks. Today, it ranks as one of the best in service, and has greatly expanded its footprint throughout Asia through acquisitions and organic growth.

It is the largest bank in Southeast Asia and has a growing presence in China and India. DBS has won multiple global banking awards, including World's Best Bank by *Euromoney*, Global Bank of the Year by *The Banker*, and Best Bank in the World by *Global Finance*. On the digital banking front, DBS was named World's Best Digital Bank by *Euromoney* twice.

Before arriving at DBS Gupta had been the CEO of Citigroup for Southeast Asia and the Pacific, but his banking roots were in operations and technology. He was a protégé of former Citi CEO John Reed, who was perhaps the first global banker to understand the importance of information and technology to the industry, and who led an information-focused transformation of Citi's back office and consumer businesses. Gupta led Transaction Services for Citi in Asia, then rose to regional head for the bank. He took a brief detour to found a dot-com business; it failed rapidly, but that indicates both his desire for innovation and willingness to fail.

Indeed, Gupta says that his earliest efforts in AI for DBS were failures, albeit instructive ones. He describes them as "signaling tools" for the organization. In 2013 Gupta signed DBS up for an AI lab with A*STAR, Singapore's primary public sector research and development organization. DBS signed a three-year contract to explore AI applications with assigned data scientists from both DBS and A*STAR. They worked on half a dozen projects, none of which were successful. But Gupta and the organization learned a lot.

As these early projects illustrate, one of Gupta's strategies for AI was simply to start with the technology early and experiment. One of the bank's key performance indicators (KPIs) was to conduct a thousand experiments a year, many of them involving AI. Gupta organized two days every six months in which the experiments were revealed to encourage employees to think more deeply on how they could deploy AI.

He also opened up the wallet to AI experimentation by giving business units and functions the flexibility to hire quasi-data scientists to see what they could accomplish. He cites the human resources team as an example of a positive outcome for this experiment. The head of HR, who had no technical background, created a skunkworks—a small, loosely structured group—to identify and pilot AI applications. The group developed JIM—the Job Intelligence Maestro application—to help the bank's recruiters hire the right talent for high-volume roles more efficiently. HR also developed an attrition prediction model. The bank derived insights such as an employee's training, revenue data, leave patterns, and more to predict the likelihood of their leaving the organization.

It's well known that data is the fuel of AI, and many companies have had to undertake substantial changes in their data environments to make them suitable for aggressive AI initiatives. What's not common is for the CEO in a large enterprise to lead the data transformation personally. Gupta credits his interest and ability to do so to his work with Citi, where he participated in the creation of that bank's first data centers and learned about data architectures.

DBS's data transformation was quite substantial. Like many firms, it moved much of its data from traditional data warehouses to data lakes—the latter is much cheaper and better suited to less-structured data. In addition, DBS created a new structure for its metadata, cleaned up eighty million incomplete data records, developed new protocols for who could access data and what customer data was suitable to capture, and introduced visualization tools to make trends in data more apparent.

Gupta continues to wrestle with the issue of where to store and process data. The bank has largely shifted to private clouds over the past several years, but there was clearly too much data to store it all on premise. They have now adopted a hybrid cloud approach, and while the move is complex, the building blocks have been put in place for the team to experiment and iterate along the way.

Under Gupta's leadership, DBS has also created new governance structures for data. It has, for example, a Responsible Data Use Committee that examines whether customer-facing data is appropriate to collect and use. The criteria applied are not just what is legal but also what would be acceptable to customers. The bank follows the mantra of PURE—data collected should be purposeful, unsurprising, respectful, and explainable.

Another area of the AI-based transformation of DBS on which Gupta has chosen to focus is the bank's talent—both professional data science talent and the many potential "citizen data scientists" across the bank. He's proud that DBS now employs around a thousand data and analytics employees, including data scientists, data analysts, and data engineers—some in a central group, but more in various functions and units around the enterprise.

For several years the bank employed participative "hackathons" for senior managers to get them to think and act on digital innovation. More recently, Gupta has looked for ideas about how to energize people and take the fear out of AI. One of his employees brought up the idea of encouraging participation in Amazon Web Service's DeepRacer League simulation, an autonomous race car game that teaches machine and reinforcement learning. DBS sought to train up to three thousand employees using this approach during 2020. Gupta himself competed and, as he put it, "I was happy to end up in the top 100 among our people." Other DBS employees did extremely well, and one was the champion in the AWS DeepRacer League F1 ProAm.

Piyush Gupta is committed to continuing to build DBS's capabilities in AI. He says that eventually the technology will be "table stakes" in the banking industry. While many other banks have employed AI capabilities from external vendors, he is committed to building AI use cases internally. "We have to have the same capabilities as the digital natives," he says. "Then we can continue to innovate and compete with them when we have to."

Gupta is committed to getting DBS people to embrace AI, and not to be scared that it might take their jobs. Thus far no one has lost employment at DBS because of AI, though some people have upskilled to change roles. Since the bank has been growing, it has been able to create substantial efficiencies with AI in certain areas (such as its customer center, using a powerful chatbot) to drive continued growth. However, Gupta admits that while he remains committed to helping his people improve their skills so that they can add value to AI, no one knows just how capable AI will be in the future.

Lessons on Leadership

What can we learn about AI leadership from this example? Gupta exhibits several traits that could be generalized to other leaders and organizations. First, it helps a lot to be familiar with information technology. A CEO who didn't have a background like Gupta's could certainly learn enough about AI and related IT infrastructure to be effective, but it would require a good deal of effort.

Second, it's important to work across multiple fronts. The specific initiatives in which a leader chooses to get involved will vary across firms, but senior executives are particularly important to signaling interest in the technology, establishing a culture of data-driven decisions, prompting innovation across the business, and motivating employees to adopt new skills.

Third, leaders hold the power of the purse. AI exploration is somewhat expensive, and AI development and production deployment is really expensive. AI leaders must invest enough to enable both levels of adoption. Note that Gupta opened the wallet for experimentation in the early days of AI adoption and didn't require a lot of financial justification. "ROI too early kills the experimentation," he argues. More recently, he has put in place KPIs for business units and functions requiring them to document the savings or returns from their AI projects. The consumer bank at DBS has a goal for this fiscal year of $50 million Singapore dollars in returns from AI, and Gupta is confident that it will be achieved.

As a final attribute, it's probably helpful for a senior AI leader to become personally engaged with some aspect of the AI-focused transformation. Data is always an important issue, though relatively few CEOs will understand it as well as Gupta did.

Another possibility for personal engagement might be the development of a particularly important AI use case. For example, Morgan Stanley's Wealth Management business—the largest in the world—built an AI-based system for recommending investment ideas to clients. The organization's chief operations officer at the time was Jim Rosenthal, and the head of Wealth Management was Andy Saperstein—now copresident of the company. Rosenthal had the idea of a Netflix-like recommendation engine more than a decade ago, and he oversaw its development until he retired from Morgan Stanley. Saperstein strongly supported the idea, and then oversaw the addition of communications platform capabilities for client engagement to what became known as the Next Best Action system. Jeff McMillan, the chief data and analytics officer at Morgan Stanley, told us that the system couldn't have been created without their long-term involvement.

There are other strong AI leaders among the AI-fueled companies we identified. Each has distinct attributes based on the context and specific needs of their businesses. At Ping An in China, for example, Peter Ma Mingzhe, a founder of the business, has a doctorate in economics and banking and takes an active role in identifying new use cases for AI in the company's multiple financial services–associated business units.

Galen G. Weston is the chairman and CEO of Loblaw, the giant Canadian retailer. Weston, like many AI leaders, is highly intellectually curious about technology and how it is reshaping the retail business. The Weston family owns most of Loblaw—and has done so for all of the company's 135-year history—and they are known to take a uniquely long-term perspective. Sarah Davis, who recently retired as the company's president, also described herself as "a very mathy person."[2]

Weston led the company's acquisition of Shoppers Drug Mart, a large pharmacy chain, and a medical records company. He is particularly focused on how data, analytics, and AI can improve the health care of the Canadian population. Loblaw already has the largest software platform for health care in the country and is providing nutrition information and healthy product recommendations for the fifty-five thousand products sold in its retail stores. Weston commented at one conference that "personalized health" is what gets him out of bed every morning.

Some of the best AI leaders are technologists at heart. As we've discussed, Gupta at DBS has strong elements of this attribute. CCC Intelligent Solutions is a midsize company that dominates the supply of data and AI-based image analysis for automobile insurance collision damage assessment. The CEO, Githesh Ramamurthy, was previously chief technology officer. As a technologist, he was able to drive the company in several critical directions based on long-term bets on how technology would evolve. The bets included:

- An early move to the cloud to store and process data across a broad ecosystem;

- An investigation and eventual implementation of collision damage image assessment based on guided photos taken by vehicle owners with their smartphones;

- Most recently, a bet that autonomous and semi-autonomous vehicle insurance will require substantial data from telematics and AI systems in the vehicle to assess damage from and culpability for an accident.

AI leadership also involves from seeing the future of a company's business and having the courage to act to achieve it. In chapter 7 we describe Deloitte's path to becoming AI fueled. Deloitte is the world's largest professional services organization, and in the past that industry has been very focused on professional human beings. But Jason Girzadas, Deloitte's Managing Principal of Businesses, Global, and

Strategic Services, is responsible for looking across all its business units and assessing their fit with the future business and economic environment. He determined that AI would play a major role in the organization's future and persuaded Deloitte's partners to invest heavily in audit, tax, consulting, and risk advisory business processes that would involve humans and AI systems working closely with each other. Deloitte doesn't claim to have fully transformed itself with AI yet, but it's off to a great start.

AI leadership takes multiple forms, but one common characteristic is that such leaders are aware of what AI can do in general, what it can do for their companies in particular, and what some of its implications might be for strategies, business models, processes, and people. Only with that understanding can they plan an effective leadership role. For much of the rest of AI leadership they can rely on the skills, intuition, and context assessment abilities they have cultivated as leaders.

Planting the Cultural Seeds for Success

For legacy companies like the ones we are describing, one of the greatest challenges to transforming with AI is to create a culture that emphasizes data-driven decisions and actions, and that is enthusiastic about the potential of AI to transform the business. Otherwise, even if there are a few AI advocates scattered around the organization, they won't get the resources they need to build great applications with the technology. Leaders of AI functions won't be able to hire great people. Even when AI applications are built, the business won't make effective use of them. In short, great AI technology without the right culture probably won't provide any value.

Some of this culture-building can be done in parallel with the pursuit of AI experiments and projects. Sometimes it also requires some level of formal education offerings. Many companies have begun data literacy or data fluency programs, in which large numbers of employees—perhaps even all of them—are trained in types of data, how that data can be used in analytics and AI programs, what types of decisions are best made with data, and how data and ways to make sense of it contribute to an organization's success. These efforts sow the seeds of success with AI by making it everyone's job to propose, develop, and implement analytics and AI tools throughout the enterprise.

Often, leading programs have multiple components. There is typically a need for conceptual learning about key aspects of data, analytics, and AI. Many people learn best from experiential learning involving perhaps a simulation or a case study discussion. After the initial training is complete, most organizations will benefit from sustainment learning that continues to reinforce key lessons and addresses new aspects of the topics.

At the level of a particular project, change management typically involves activities such as identifying stakeholders, gaining clarity about objectives and performance expectations for the AI system, communicating frequently about project progress and demonstrating prototypes to get feedback, and retraining/upskilling workers who will be users of the new system. Since data scientists and AI experts are often less interested in such activities compared to building models and programming them, many companies are putting AI project or product managers in place to ensure that change management activities are given their due.

Survey data supports the importance of this type of intervention. Organizations that invest in change management to a high degree are 1.6 times as likely to report that AI initiatives exceed expectations and more than 1.5 times as likely to achieve their desired goals, compared to the rest of the surveyed companies.[3] Deloitte is following its own thought leadership and advice in this regard. In 2021 it launched the Deloitte AI Academy to create and scale AI talent. The aspiration of the academy is not only to train its own professionals on AI but also to be a creator of AI talent in the broader economy.

For leaders of analytics and AI functions, evangelism and cultural transformation about AI may be the single most important role they play in bringing about success with the technology. Disney's analytics and AI organization even uses the term *evangelytics* to emphasize the importance of communicating about and persuading various audiences within a company about the virtues of analytics and AI as business tools. If your company is lucky enough not to need much evangelism about data and AI (though that is unlikely), you can focus on implementation.

The steps that leaders of AI groups can take while identifying, experimenting with, and implementing AI systems are like those for other relatively new technologies. It's advisable, for example, to leverage early adopters and go where interest is high. For example, at Bank of Montreal, Ren Zhang, until recently the head of their AI Center of Excellence, focused initially on AI use cases in businesses with a lot of data.[4] The bank's digital unit, for example, has large volumes of clickstream data from customers and needs AI and analytics to make sense of the data and to personalize customer interactions. The bank's financial crimes unit also has data on customer and employee behaviors and is always interested in using the latest AI tools to identify and stop criminal activity. Zhang focused her AI initiatives somewhat less on the more conservative parts of the business. The commercial bank, for example, serves fewer customers than the consumer bank and prefers a personal touch over more automated processes and interactions. Executives in the credit risk function support using data and analytics for better credit decisions, but that aspect of the business is heavily regulated.

Leaders of AI projects should solicit and take advantage of support from business leaders. That will both ensure needed resources and persuade the rest of the company that the management team is behind AI projects. Ideally, this would be done prior to starting large AI initiatives. For example, when Vipin Gopal was offered the job of chief data and analytics officer at Eli Lilly (which is doing interesting and useful work with AI), one of his first activities was to interview business leaders across the organization. Out of the interviews, he recommended three areas to focus on for use cases. For each case, he discussed the costs and benefits with the leader of the area and presented the ideas to the entire senior executive team. The projects were all endorsed and are moving ahead successfully. Some have already shown considerable benefits in partial implementation. Of course, the more aggressive the approach to AI, the more important it is to ensure that stakeholders are solidly behind the effort.

Another aspect of aligning the organization behind AI is to communicate results and publicize successes often. As mentioned previously, Piyush Gupta at DBS encouraged the organization of events where successful or promising AI experiments were showcased a couple of times a year. Gopal at Lilly also stages events of this type—not only to publicize results, but to build a community of data- and AI-focused people around the company. Particularly when these employees are in decentralized organizational structures, it's important to get them together fairly often—once a year at least. These events can focus on both community-building and learning about new AI-related skills and technologies.

For people who lead AI efforts within companies, it's important to maintain a positive view of AI by combining short-term value with long-term transformation potential. Many executives—if we believe our own and other organizations' surveys—believe that AI will have a transformational effect on their businesses and industries. In the 2020 survey, for example, 75 percent of the global executives surveyed, all of whom had adopted AI, believed that it would transform their organizations quickly—within three years.[5]

To help meet those expectations, AI developers should produce great use cases and production deployments of applications. Yet, as we've discussed, today's AI is relatively narrow, and it's not generally capable of handling even entire jobs by itself, much less entire business processes. So leaders of AI organizations will have to publicize small successes and put them in the context of the transformational changes they will help to enable.

For example, at one AI-focused health insurer we've worked with, the AI group used a machine learning application to extract member data from PDF files. This seems like a rather pedestrian accomplishment, but it was described to the relevant stakeholders as a step toward the transformation of customer interaction. Extracting data from the PDFs meant that call center reps could use the data to quickly determine the details of a member's health plan and answer questions much more easily. It was also a stepping-stone toward a conversational AI system that would eventually reduce the need for call center calls. The head of AI, in discussing the system, emphasized both the short-term accomplishment and the longer-term plans.

Educating Employees about AI and Their Future Work

Perhaps the most logistically challenging among the human side of AI issues is educating employees about its capabilities and likely future impact on their jobs. It's difficult for a variety of reasons: there are many employees within a large organization; it's hard to predict what changes in jobs will take place because of AI over the next several years; and finally, different employees have different objectives and interests relative to their jobs, so "one size fits all" educational initiatives are unlikely to be successful.

Some companies—generally not those that are all-in on AI—have taken these challenges as a reason to limit educating their employees about AI.[6] One large defense contractor's HR leadership, for example, justified their approach with three arguments:

1. The company has many other competing priorities in the near term. Is it worth investing in something that is so long-term and uncertain in its impact?

2. Job changes and automation are moving a lot more slowly than the experts predicted. We'll be able to adjust as the

changes come. When jobs do change, most of the time it's task augmentation or new skills rather than layoffs. That kind of change is less difficult to accomplish and easier to plan for.

3. There's so much uncertainty around the prognostication that we're likely to be wrong. Then the company will need to do real-time adjusting anyway.

Although these arguments are reasonable, we take a different view. We believe it is possible to predict some changes in jobs from AI, or at least to better equip employees to prepare for more generic job changes. And while it's true that augmentation is more likely than large-scale automation, augmentation will likely lead to job changes for which workers need to be prepared. Our 2018 survey of AI adopters found that 82 percent expected moderate or substantial job changes for their employees in three years.[7] Despite competing priorities, we believe the time is now to educate employees about AI and its impacts. It's likely to take a while, so there is little time to waste. These happen to be the same ideas that some AI-focused companies are using to justify their present actions.

Of course, some organizations that want to retrain or upskill workers aren't certain what specific skills will be required for jobs of the future, but they are confident that those skills will be digitally oriented. Amazon, for instance, has committed to spend $700 million on retraining to ensure that its employees have the skills they will need to thrive in an increasingly digital job market—within or outside Amazon. The company's primary focus is the third of its workers in distribution centers, its transportation network, and nontechnical roles at headquarters. It provides retraining for workers in distribution centers (which are more vulnerable to automation) for jobs as IT support technicians, and for nontechnical corporate workers in software engineering skills.[8]

Similarly, leaders at DBS Bank in Singapore provided employees with seven digital skills, including digital communications, digital business models, digital technologies, and data-driven thinking. The program is called DigiFY, and it is aimed at upskilling many of the bank's employees. Deloitte has focused on making its professionals tech savvy—assuming that in an AI-oriented business environment, virtually every employee will need to understand how technology works and fits with their jobs. All three companies believe that whatever changes happen to future jobs, employees—and their employers—will be better off if they are more skilled at digital technologies.

Sometimes these new skills lead to a new set of roles. DBS also created a group of "translators"—people who are quantitatively oriented, but not data scientists, and who can mediate between business stakeholders and AI developers.[9] This role is an important one that has been fairly widely discussed, but not widely implemented. DBS has even decided to staff AI projects with one translator for every two data scientists. Sameer Gupta, the bank's chief analytics officer, said that when the two roles collaborate, data scientists can be more experimental with their modeling, while the translator can ensure that the actual business problem is being specifically addressed.

A variation on this strategy is to educate employees in data science skills. This approach often involves working with the providers of online courses in that area. Shell, for example, began a relationship with Udacity in 2019, when the energy giant realized it had nowhere near the number of data scientists needed to complete all the AI-related projects it planned. It created a pilot program for people with IT backgrounds and then embarked on a larger initiative aimed at petroleum engineers, chemists, data scientists, and geophysicists, among others. Completing the AI nanodegree typically takes four to six months to finish, working ten to fifteen hours per week. As of this writing, more than five hundred employees had completed or were currently enrolled in the nanodegree program, and an additional one thousand staff had completed data literacy and digital literacy courses.

Similarly, Airbus has partnered with Udacity to train more than a thousand employees in data science and analytics. The company asks both employees and their managers to devote half a day a week to the training. Managers work with employees to identify a pilot project in data science the employees can work on, and the managers monitor their progress. Airbus believes the training initiative has multiple benefits. It has not only increased the number of people who can work with AI but has also led to a community of people who are interested in data science and AI with whom the central data science group can collaborate. The training program is also a means to deploy AI best practices around the company, and the projects are a way to familiarize managers and their businesses with AI.

Some organizations are attempting to predict the nature of future jobs and the skills they will require. This is, of course, difficult or impossible to do with any precision. Even if predictions are possible, they will probably differ substantially from job to job. Nevertheless, these companies are embarking on approaches that predict the future of all jobs in the organization, those that are particularly likely to be affected by AI, or jobs that are closely tied to future strategies.

One large US bank, for example—an aggressive adopter of AI—has announced a $350 million investment in reskilling related to AI-related job changes, and the bank is being both predictive and granular about the initiative.[10] It's working with researchers from MIT and elsewhere to understand—based on a "suitability for machine learning" (SML) assessment—which skills and jobs are most likely to be replaced by AI.[11] The SML analysis will help the bank plan for changes in those jobs and help workers gain the skills they need to succeed in their modified jobs or transition to new ones. Some companies are making specific job predictions based on their strategies or products. In Europe, a consortium of microelectronics companies, the Euro Pact for Skills, is devoting €2 billion to train current and future employees on electronic components and systems. General Motors is training its employees to manufacture electric and autonomous vehicles. Verizon is hiring and training data scientists and marketers to expand its 5G wireless technology. SAP is growing employees' skills in cloud computing, artificial intelligence development, blockchain, and the internet of things. Predictions about industry-specific trends and directions that guide employee reskilling are easier than for business in general, although they, too, could go awry.

Unilever, a company that is relying heavily on AI for its present and future, is taking a different approach to preparing workers for future jobs. Instead of trying to predict which jobs will change, the company is helping workers take more ownership of their own career paths. Employees are empowered to make the changes they want to make in their jobs and careers rather than waiting to react to changes imposed on them. Unilever facilitates this process by describing alternative career progressions. The company helps workers choose target occupations and understand the skills needed to attain them. Then Unilever provides a wide range of training options—both internal and external—to gain those skills.

Similarly, one of the most popular HR tools at GE Digital—an early adopter of AI for manufacturing applications—shows workers which jobs in the company are natural next steps from the ones they have now.[12] Employees can look privately at the tool to see possible paths they can follow, skills they may need to acquire, or even positions that are open. This helps employees feel that they have more opportunities and that they have more control over their positions in the company.

Education of any type on AI and related issues is probably a good thing, but it is often best when it is engaging to the participants— for anyone, but particularly for executives. Several companies have created programs that involve active investigation and development of AI-related projects for senior managers. DBS, for example, created "hackathons" in which the goal was less to write a program and more to think about all the elements that would go into an AI-oriented product or service. TD Bank's Wealth Management business unit had a similar program, WealthACT (Accelerate Change Through Technology), that included visits to tech centers like Silicon Valley, Boston, and Montreal and involved interviews with customers and development of new products.[13]

It's clear that AI-powered companies have gotten the message that AI is not just about technology: they are propelled by strong leaders, they are building data-driven cultures, and they are educating their people to actively participate in their AI journeys. Most of them would likely attest to the fact that AI technology is the easy part; getting people and organizations mobilized to explore, build, and use it is the challenge. But these aggressive adopters of AI have largely succeeded in that objective, and they can be a model for other organizations that wish to take AI seriously as a competitive weapon and tool for business transformation.

CHAPTER 3

Strategy

If you do not have a vision of your organization's AI strategy,
then you are not prepared for the next wave of technological
disruption. . . . You will need to decide what role your company
will play in the next technological wave and how you will
integrate AI into your business to be a leader in your industry.

—written autonomously by the Megatron
AI system from Nvidia

We often think of AI as the primary province of data scientists and technologists, who are needed to train and deploy AI models. But in organizations transforming themselves with AI, we also need a different group of people to be involved and a different set of conversations to take place. Companies should increasingly be asking, "How can AI improve our business?" "What can we do with AI to create new offerings to help us grow?" "How can we make money with AI?" These questions, which are definitely being asked and answered in AI-fueled companies, are strategy conversations that need to be conducted among senior managers, strategy departments, even strategy consultants.

Of course, these conversations can be challenging. They require both a knowledge of business situations and strategic possibilities, and a knowledge of how AI might address or transform them. That's why "conversations" is the right word—no single individual can have all the ideas, and the ideas will be refined with discussion and deliberation.

There are three major strategic archetypes for what an organization is attempting to accomplish with AI. Any AI strategy should be considered in the context of the archetype they hope to achieve. The archetypes include:

- *Creating something new*, including new businesses or markets, new business models or ecosystems, new products, and/or new services;

- *Transforming operations*, becoming dramatically more efficient and effective at the company's existing strategy;

- *Influencing customer behavior* using AI to influence a critical behavior of customers, such as how they socialize, maintain their health, live their financial lives, drive their vehicles, and so forth.

In this chapter we'll describe a series of topics involving the strategic impacts of AI, and look at some examples of companies addressing each of those strategic archetypes. The AI-focused companies we'll discuss include:

- For new businesses and markets: Loblaw

- For new products and services: Toyota and Morgan Stanley

- For new business models and ecosystems: Ping An, Airbus, Shell, SOMPO, and Anthem

- For transforming operations: the Kroger Co.

- For influencing customer behavior: a variety of companies including FICO, Manulife, Progressive Insurance, and Well

Several of these companies are pursuing more than one strategic archetype with AI at once. We'll focus, however, on the primary archetype they are trying to achieve.

Strategy Archetype 1: Creating Something New

AI enables the creation of several new ways of doing business in all-in companies. That might involve new businesses and markets, new products and services, and—perhaps the most exciting opportunity from AI—new business models and ecosystems. We'll describe each of these approaches to creating something new and provide a detailed example (or several in some cases) of companies that have adopted them.

New businesses and markets

All-in on AI companies employ AI not only to support their existing businesses, but also to facilitate new business creation and entry into new markets. They build on existing strengths with AI to offer new types of products and services, or to offer existing ones in a more efficient and effective fashion. Though we think this is a good idea, our annual "AI in the Enterprise" survey results over several years suggest that most companies use AI to improve existing business processes. However, the 2021 survey found that lower-achieving organizations (called starters and underachievers) tended to focus more on efficiency or cost-out goals, while high-achieving organizations (called transformers and pathseekers) were more likely to emphasize growth-oriented goals, such as improving customer satisfaction, creating new products and offers, and entering new markets. Further evidence of the value of innovative strategic thinking on AI comes from a recent *MIT Sloan Management Review* analysis, which found that companies that use AI primarily to explore and create new forms of business value are 2.7 times more likely to improve their ability to compete with AI than those who use AI primarily to improve existing processes.[1]

Loblaw is using AI to fuel its growth in the health-care industry. Best known for its retail grocery stores—it is the largest grocery chain in Canada—Loblaw has been moving aggressively into health care. In 2013 it acquired Shoppers Drug Mart, the largest pharmacy chain in Canada. In 2017 it bought electronic medical records provider QHR. In 2020 it made a minority investment in telemedicine provider Maple. The company has over two thousand locations through which it can offer health-care services, and over 150 clinics.

However, company leaders often remark that "the future of health care is digital," and much of that orientation is focused on the PC Health app (PC, or President's Choice, is Loblaw's high-performing upscale retail store brand). PC Health isn't designed to replace existing health-care services in Canada, most of which are nationalized. Instead, it is intended to help Canadians navigate effectively through the health-care system and provide a "front door" to health services. Loblaw also offers Canada's largest loyalty program, and PC Health users can win loyalty points for health-oriented activities. In the future, Loblaw plans to integrate PC Health with data from wearable and home medical devices, and to reward healthy behaviors with loyalty points.

Much of the AI in PC Health is available through a partnership with League, a Canadian startup that provides personalized health recommendations and tailored programs for specific health objectives. League also works with employers and insurance companies.

Although League makes use of AI to provide personalized recommendations, both it and Loblaw are committed to offering human health-care advice as well—from pharmacists, nurses, and doctors.

Loblaw's data assets in health care are robust. It has electronic medical records, pharmacy prescription data, and even a broad collection of medical imaging data. And it knows what foods many of its customers purchase at their grocery stores. Given their positive experience so far, it seems likely that Loblaw will continue to provide new health-care offerings based on AI.

New products and services

Another strategic use of AI is to create new products and services, or provide significant enhancements to existing ones. This is a familiar trend among Silicon Valley companies, which have added AI to many products. At Google, for example, AI is embedded in search, Gmail, Maps, Home, Translate, and many other products. But as we've suggested, adding AI to products comes naturally to digital native organizations. It is often much more challenging for legacy companies to add AI to their products and services in a meaningful way.

AI in new products: autonomous vehicles

Perhaps the most obvious example of adding AI to a physical product is autonomous vehicles. Unfortunately, there have been some problems with the concept of fully autonomous driving. In fact, the automobile world is in quiet retreat on the topic of fully autonomous vehicles. Vehicle autonomy is closely linked with ride-sharing, and in the pandemic era of the early 2020s, customers seem less interested in sharing vehicles.[2] Several manufacturers of autonomous vehicles have claimed self-driving capabilities for robo-taxis and private vehicles, but these have been discontinued or delayed—in some cases multiple times. Starsky Robotics, an autonomous truck startup, went out of business. As *Car and Driver* put it in the title of a recent article, "Self-Driving Cars Are Taking Longer to Build Than Everyone Thought."[3]

The consensus in the industry seems to be that we are 80 percent of the way toward self-driving cars, but that the remaining 20 percent will take as long as the initial 80 percent did—which was about forty years. Self-driving cars are thriving in some highly constrained environments—geofenced, pedestrian-free zones in cities in warm, dry cities like Phoenix, for example, where Google/Waymo robo-taxis ply a defined set of streets—but these restricted settings may not have enough vehicles to allow the industry to prosper.

Toyota's strategy on smart cars could be an interesting one. Toyota isn't necessarily the first name that comes up in the list of autonomous vehicle developers, or even of AI-focused companies in general. But for years it's been pursuing Guardian—an AI-focused project at Toyota Research Institute (TRI) focused on making human driving smarter and safer. Gill Pratt, the CEO of TRI, has emphasized safety for several years now. After Pratt spoke at an MIT conference on autonomous vehicles in 2017, Tom wrote:

> He [Pratt] pointed out, for example, that although less than 1 percent of adult deaths in the United States are from auto accidents, 35 percent of teenage deaths are. So Toyota is trying to develop a vehicle with a "Guardian" mode to protect teens (and other bad drivers, presumably) from making lethal driving mistakes. The company is also working on a "Chauffeur" mode for older drivers who need continuous help—particularly important in Japan, with its rapidly aging population.[4]

Pratt and TRI are still working on both the Guardian and Chauffeur projects. It's difficult to know how far along they are, although a TRI job description contained this information:

Join us in our mission to improve the quality of human life through advances in artificial intelligence, automated driving, robotics, and materials science. We're dedicated to building a world of "mobility for all" where everyone, regardless of age or ability, can live in harmony with technology to enjoy a better life. Through innovations in AI, we'll help

- Develop vehicles incapable of causing a crash, regardless of the actions of the driver.

- Develop technology for vehicles and robots to help people enjoy new levels of independence, access, and mobility.

- Bring advanced mobility technology to market faster.

- Discover new materials that will make batteries and hydrogen fuel cells smaller, lighter, less expensive and more powerful. [NB: this research at TRI also draws extensively on AI]

- Develop human-centered AI systems to augment (not replace) human decision-making to increase the quality of decisions (e.g., mitigate cognitive biases) and/or to facilitate faster innovation cycles.[5]

Toyota did reveal some specific information on Guardian at the 2019 Consumer Electronics Show, where a press release described a "blended envelope control" approach to improving safety.[6] The details remain to be seen, but it appears to be a drive-by-wire (digital controls) situation where the driver provides inputs to the car's computers, and the computer can override those inputs if they seem dangerous. According to Toyota, this approach is similar to how a modern fighter jet works.

It's too early to say how drivers will react to having their cars veto their intentions; this may be a bit more intelligence and control than some drivers want. But most drivers don't seem to have reacted too negatively to lane change warnings that vibrate the steering wheel, or autonomous braking systems that take over when they sense an object in the way at close range. The more aggressive Guardian system may simply be viewed as an extension of those driver augmentations.

Of course, this is all just a strategy. The implementation will make all the difference to the eventual success or failure of the Guardian approach. And just in case, Toyota and TRI are also working on Chauffeur—the full autonomy approach—although the company suggests that it has recently focused primarily on Guardian. Pratt stated that the safety features will be available "in the 2020s," which seems far more realistic than imminent predictions about full autonomy. Toyota has another advanced driver assistance system brand called Teammate, which is being introduced on some 2022 models. It offers semi-autonomous cruise and parking capabilities.

We see many reasons why this strategy is a good one for Toyota. The company is known for producing highly reliable vehicles that gradually but steadily improve each year—using the Toyota Production System—and this approach to vehicle intelligence fits well into that company culture. The safety focus is also more likely to provide some economic returns well before full autonomy does. Automakers and venture capital firms have invested more than $16 billion in full autonomy projects, but short-term returns on all that money seem unlikely. But a safety-oriented parent or older driver might purchase a Toyota because of its Guardian features. Adding AI-based autonomy or increased driver safety to cars is a long-term play to be sure, but Toyota's Guardian approach to incorporating AI in vehicles seems a better short-term bet than the full autonomy ones.

Similarly, Airbus has been working for several years on visual navigation capabilities for airplanes and helicopters, including the taxi, takeoff, and landing activities that have not historically been included in automatic pilot systems of aircraft. While Airbus has implemented autonomous air travel of various types, it has no intention of replacing human pilots with these AI tools. Instead, its focus is on pilot assistance and enhanced safety.

AI in new services: wealth management

AI can also be used to differentiate and add value in services. That often means delivering the same services as before, but providing them in a different, more intelligent way. For example, more than ten years ago, Jim Rosenthal, then chief operating officer at Morgan Stanley, had the idea that a Netflix-like recommendation engine could help Morgan Stanley's wealth management group differentiate its wealth management offerings. Morgan Stanley has a big wealth practice—ranked third in the world after UBS and Credit Suisse in assets under management—and it was traditionally focused on using human financial advisors to advise clients.[7]

Since Rosenthal came up with the recommendation idea, Morgan Stanley has been working on a next-best-action (NBA) system to provide its advisors with financial insights to present to clients. The company tried a variety of AI technologies and settled on machine learning to identify investments, actions of interest, and relevance to a particular client. When the system was originally introduced in 2017, the sole focus was on creating personalized investment offers. The NBA system allows the financial advisor to identify a personalized investing idea for a client in seconds—a task that previously required about forty-five minutes. The manual approach isn't really feasible when the average financial advisor has two hundred or so clients.

The NBA system might recommend twenty or so possible ideas to send to a client in a particular day, but the financial advisor decides whether to send them. It might, for example, tell a client with a particular bond that its rating has been downgraded and recommend an alternative. It might also say that their advisor noticed that the client has just added $100,000 to their account, and to contact the financial advisor to discuss ideas for investing it. If a mutual fund or exchange-traded fund has a change in management, the system might suggest contacting the client to discuss whether to stay with the fund. Near the end of the tax year, it might suggest some tax planning considerations to suggest to the client. In this context, the NBA system is used to transition a client to a more actively managed portfolio.

Morgan Stanley's NBA system also makes recommendations on the risk level and issues within a portfolio based on a partnership with BlackRock and its Aladdin Wealth risk management platform. It screens client portfolios for various types of risk on an ongoing basis. If Aladdin discovers a high level of risk, the client is notified and encouraged to discuss it with their financial advisor.

Since 2017 Morgan Stanley has also focused on the client engagement and communications aspects of the NBA system. The Wealth Management unit's management team has concluded that the primary way a financial advisor achieves success is by frequent engagement with the client. And the Next Best Action system, which now includes a client communications platform, facilitates that process. As Jeff McMillan, the chief analytics officer for the business, put it in an interview, "We have a very sophisticated machine learning algorithm to identify topics of interest to clients. But in the end financial advising is a human-based game. If all the system does is remind them that the advisor is there and looking out for them, that is often enough."

Usage of the system is voluntary—and not all financial advisors use it—so it is impossible to attribute assets under management or other financial measures to the NBA system or the communications platform. But McMillan said that advisors who use it are both more efficient—because coming up with relevant investing ideas is much quicker with the system—and their clients are more engaged. It was particularly helpful during the Covid-19 pandemic, when financial advisors sent out over eleven million messages to clients in just the first two months of the lockdown. Advisors couldn't see clients face-to-face, but they could engage with them online.

Other high-end wealth management companies sometimes say that AI isn't capable of managing client portfolios that include alternative investments, such as art, commodities, or private equity. But McMillan told us that's not a good excuse:

> There is the perception that these tools are only suitable for the "mass affluent" segment, and not the ultra high net worth space. The argument is that the populations are too small for trustworthy recommendations. But we can drive specific opportunities based on individualized client behavior and characteristics. If there's not enough data for machine learning, we can use business rules, or a test-and-control approach to see what's generating response.

McMillan commented that this is not a system, but a way of doing business that would be difficult for competitors to replicate. He credits a cross-functional approach to managing the system and the process, and executives who were far-sighted and stuck with the idea over time. In addition to Rosenthal, who is now retired, McMillan credits Andy Saperstein, former head of Wealth Management and now copresident of Morgan Stanley. In our view McMillan deserves a lot of credit as well for making the NBA system a reality.

New business models and ecosystems

AI has been enabling new strategies and business models for the last couple of decades, although most of the companies benefiting from them have been digital native companies. Of course, it worked out well for them; their multisided platforms—in which they manage relationships between buyers and sellers—have been fast-growing and very profitable. The consultant Barry Libert's research on business model types has shown that multisided platforms have the highest valuations of any business model—more than four times the annual revenue multiples attached to some legacy business models.[8]

AI plays an important role in making platform business models work. Data comes from all participants in the platform, and machine learning helps match customers with the products and services they need or want. Customer offerings can be personalized with AI. And the millions of customers that use platforms need highly efficient customer service like that provided by intelligent agents and chatbots. It's not surprising, then, that Facebook, Airbnb, Amazon, Google, Uber, Alibaba, Tencent, and the other leading platform users are also world leaders in the application of AI to their businesses.

But AI-fueled companies in legacy businesses are also beginning to develop platform-based business models driven by AI. They are adding new businesses and creating new business ecosystems in order to grow, gather data, and attract and serve new customers.[9] For them, AI becomes a primary means of reducing friction for customers. Evidence that AI leaders take an ecosystem approach comes from our 2021 survey, which found that organizations with more diverse ecosystems were 1.4 times as likely to use AI in a way that differentiates them from their competitors. In addition, the two highest achieving groups of AI users in the survey, called transformers and pathseekers, were substantially more likely to have two or more ecosystem relationships (83 percent among the two highest groups, versus 70 percent and 59 percent among the two lowest groups). Organizations with diverse ecosystems were also significantly more likely to have a transformative vision for AI, to have enterprise-wide AI strategies, and to use AI as a strategic differentiator. These survey findings don't necessarily involve full-fledged platforms, but creating an ecosystem is a first step toward that capability.

AI-driven ecosystems: Ping An

Perhaps the single best example of an AI-driven ecosystem is Ping An in China, which began as an insurance company in 1988 but now describes itself as a leading consumer financial services company offering products and services across an integrated financial services platform. Its businesses include financial services, health care, auto services, and smart cities services.

In health care, for example, Ping An's health-care ecosystem connects government, patients, medical service providers, health insurers, and technology. In health-care services, it uses AI-related services to help doctors diagnose and treat conditions covering more than two thousand diseases. As of September 2021, the operation had served 400 million users, providing 1.2 billion cumulative consultations using an in-house medical team numbering 2,000 and, in addition, more than 46,500 external doctors. It partners with 189,000 pharmacies, 4,000 hospitals, and 83,000 medical institutions. These numbers illustrate not only the size of China's population, but also the rapid scaling possible with a digital platform business model.

While the primary value of this ecosystem is to grow the business and provide effective health care, it's also critical for accumulating insights to train AI models. With the appropriate permissions and authorizations, the Ping An health-care ecosystem can draw claims and payments data from payers, treatment data from care providers, prescription data from pharmacies, symptom data from patients, and other types of data from other ecosystem members. By 2020 Ping An had data on more than thirty thousand diseases and more than a billion medical consultation records. Altogether, Ping An's business model comprises what Jing Xiao, the company's chief scientist, calls "a deep ocean of data."

Ping An also offers radiology image analysis services through its Ping An smart health-care unit, which is part of its smart cities ecosystem. Its image reading system has shortened diagnosis times that assist doctors and medical consultants from fifteen minutes to fifteen seconds. It also allows Ping An to gather more labeled images, which helps to improve its image analysis machine learning models.

We could describe similar synergies and growth across the other ecosystems. And the health care/smart city relationship is only one example of Ping An's strategy to develop an ecosystem of ecosystems. In 2020, for example, 36 percent of its 37 million new customers were obtained through its ecosystems. As of June 2021, nearly 62 percent of Ping An's more than 223 million retail customers used services from the health-care ecosystem. On average, these customers have more accounts and more assets than its other customers. Ping An says it is pursuing further connections between the lifestyle financial services and health-care services ecosystems.

Emerging new ecosystems at Airbus, Shell, and SOMPO

Several of the other AI-powered companies we've identified are also pursuing ecosystems and platforms, but are in earlier stages than Ping An. At this point they are still exploring business and revenue models, but are pursuing data sharing and integration approaches, and beginning to develop AI applications to analyze the data.

Airbus, for example, launched Skywise in 2017. The open data platform was established in collaboration with Palantir Technologies. The objective was to become the platform of reference used by all major aviation players to improve their operational performance and business results and to support their own digital transformations. Current commercial aircraft can produce more than thirty gigabytes of data per day, measuring more than forty thousand operational parameters around the aircraft. By 2021, Skywise had more than 140 airlines and over 9,500 connected aircraft.

Since Skywise's launch Airbus's analytics and AI experts have developed a series of additional applications that take advantage of all the available data: Skywise Health Monitoring, Skywise Predictive Maintenance, and Skywise Reliability. The goal of all these

applications is to improve fleet performance and ultimately to erad-
icate unscheduled maintenance.

Health monitoring integrates all data from the aircraft in real
time. It analyzes and prioritizes equipment events, allowing quicker
decision-making. It can also assist with decisions on where to find
needed parts. Predictive maintenance, as used in many other industries, uses data and machine learning to predict when aircraft components need to be serviced, as opposed to servicing at fixed intervals.
Reliability provides detailed metrics on equipment and can identify
and prioritize technical issues across a fleet of aircraft. Airbus also
maintains a global tracking dataset to which airlines can subscribe
to track their own and other operators' planes around the world.

Airbus has built an even more open ecosystem in its Defense and
Space division with its OneAtlas satellite imagery and analytics service. Its satellites take the images, and its deep learning models
(developed by Airbus and its partners) allow users to detect and classify objects, and identify changes over time. These very accurate
geospatial analytics range from land use and change detection, to
economic activity analysis and monitoring. Such capabilities can be
further used as building blocks to develop thematic services for some
verticals such as defense, mapping, agriculture, forestry, and oil and
gas. They can either be completely Airbus made, like Starling (defor-
estation) and Ocean Finder (maritime), or developed with deep
industry expertise partners: Preligens for defense site monitoring,
which automatically monitors hundreds of sensitive sites worldwide
and produces automatic detection reports; Orbital Insight for Earth
Monitor, to detect changes in infrastructure and land use in near
real-time, as well as to identify and count cars, trucks, and aircraft;
4 Earth Intelligence to analyze air quality and map terrestrial and
marine habitats; or Sinergise and the Euro Data Cube for analytics
that measure the impact of Covid-19 on the European economy and
society. Romaric Redon, who leads AI planning and strategy for
Airbus at group level, commented in an interview with us, "The
diversity of what can be done with OneAtlas space imagery goes far

beyond what Airbus can do alone. So, the approach is to build an open ecosystem with the right building blocks for enabling further applications development by great partners."

Another AI-oriented company that has established several ecosystems—also in partnership with Palantir, in which it has made a substantial investment—is SOMPO Holdings, a large insurance and elder care company based in Japan. SOMPO has a strategic objective to use data and AI to deliver societal transformation in security, health, and well-being. With that in mind, it has recently established not one ecosystem but five:

- mobility (automobile insurance has long been a company focus);

- nursing care (it is the largest owner and operator of nursing homes in Japan);

- healthy aging (an important issue given Japan's demographic situation);

- resilience as a service (for businesses and government);

- agriculture (its SOMPO International subsidiary provides crop and weather insurance).

Koichi Narasaki, the head of these ecosystems and SOMPO's chief digital officer, told us that in each area the company expects to use Palantir approaches for data integration across participating companies in the ecosystems, which will include both competitors and partners. SOMPO will develop AI applications to analyze and add value to the data. It has been pursuing AI since 2015 and has a number of applications in place for mobility and nursing care. The company also expects to get AI help from investments it has made in startups, such as Abeja, a Japanese deep learning startup, and One Concern, a US startup with an AI-based "resilience platform." It has also formed a new digital subsidiary—SOMPO Light Vortex— for the sale of digital and AI applications to other companies.

Shell is also establishing a new ecosystem focused on AI-based transformation of the energy industry.[10] Called the Open AI Energy Initiative, its goal is to make the energy industry and other large industrial organizations more efficient with AI, with a particular focus on reliability solutions. The technology partners in the ecosystem thus far are C3.AI, a software and services vendor with a focus on industrial AI applications; Microsoft, which will incorporate cloud services; and Baker Hughes, a leading energy technology and oil field services company.

Each of the initial partners and subsequent ecosystem members will supply AI applications and capabilities to the initiative. The arrangement is barter style: AI offerings are the key to participation through a fair value exchange. Each application that is accepted by the initiative will run on the C3.AI platform and will ultimately resemble, as Dan Jeavons, the head of digital innovation and computational science at Shell, put it, "an app store for the process industry." Jeavons also said that the ecosystem also plans to share data: "The rich data assets that operators have built up over many years are critical to solving some of the toughest digital problems," and the initiative has "a standardized data model based on open standards."[11]

It isn't yet clear what the commercial implications of the Open AI Energy Initiative will be for its members, and maintenance is a relatively narrow business process compared to those addressed by some of the other AI-driven ecosystems. Collaboration on maintenance would probably not raise antitrust concerns. However, the initiative is expanding to encompass issues like how energy companies can transform to sustainable energy sources, optimize the development of oil and gas fields, and reduce leakages from pipelines and wells.

A digital platform for health at Anthem, Inc.

Another AI-fueled organization that has embraced the idea of a platform-based business model is Anthem, Inc., a leading health company dedicated to improving communities, and serving more than forty-five million consumers within its family of health plans. Anthem has been working on a digital and AI-enabled strategy for several years, and part of its goal—rather than to provide health-care services itself, as some of its competitors are doing—is to connect its members digitally with the health-care providers and services they need—determined, in part, by AI.

Gail Boudreaux, Anthem's CEO, has spoken publicly about this strategy. At the company's 2021 Investors Conference, she said:

> The traditional insurance company that we were, has given way to the digitally enabled platform for health we are becoming. . . . This platform strategy is grounded in data and deploys predictive analytics, artificial intelligence, machine learning and collaboration across the value chain to produce proactive, personalized solutions for our consumers, care providers, employers and communities. By leveraging these digital capabilities, we will build upon our broad Anthem portfolio of pharmacy, behavioral, clinical and complex care assets and algorithms to deliver integrated whole person health solutions. Not only will our digital platform and diversified assets support and accelerate the growth of Anthem internally, but also increasingly look to meet the growing needs of our external customers and partners.

The shift to a digital platform for health is a long-term journey for Anthem, but the company has already delivered on some AI-enabled functionality. Anthem stood up a company called Hydrogen Health, in partnership with Blackstone and K Health, to create a symptom checker app for mobile phones that provides members with knowledge about how other people with similar symptoms were diagnosed and treated. The app then suggests whether members should consult with a doctor. If they do, it provides low-cost access to a telehealth consultation; if they do not, it provides options for self-treatment or other ways to learn more. As of 2021, there had been over 52,000 interactions with the symptom checker.

Anthem is also pursuing an additional strategic archetype—that of influencing the behavior of its customers or members to help them live healthier lives. One way it is doing this is through a partnership with Lark, a startup that offers health counseling integrated with Anthem's smartphone app based on personalized recommendations and conversational AI. The app sends text messages with recommended actions for diabetes, cardiovascular disease, prediabetes, smoking cessation, stress, anxiety, and weight management. It securely uses data from Anthem's member claims as well as from connected medical devices such as blood pressure cuffs, scales, and glucose meters for remote monitoring. If necessary, Lark arranges a live telephone conversation with a human health coach. Over two million patients are receiving Lark's recommendations, and research has established that lifestyle interventions can deliver impressive results in various clinical domains, such as blood sugar reduction and diabetes prevention.[12]

Dealmaking versus developing in ecosystem-based AI

For most of these ecosystems (Ping An is an exception), there has been more dealmaking than actual development of AI applications, and the early focus has been on integrating data across organizational boundaries. In order to make these ecosystems and associated business models successful, the companies involved will need to:

- build substantial internal capabilities to develop AI applications;

- partner with external vendors of AI capabilities that can be applied to their problems;

- work out the collaboration vs. competition issues that arise among ecosystem members who are traditional competitors;

- determine how to allocate the financial benefits from new business models.

In short, there is both more dealmaking and more developing to be done. Given the uncertainties of this activity, as well as of possible external inputs—for example, potential regulatory interventions and limitations—it's difficult to know how these ecosystems will play out over time. However, given the success of Ping An's business model, it is certainly possible that AI-driven ecosystems will play a major role in the global economy of the near future.

Strategy Archetype 2: Transforming Operations

In addition to facilitating new strategies, new markets, and new business models, AI can simply be used to transform operations—to make existing and well-defined strategies much more successful. If a company wants its supply chain managers to make products show up on time, its marketers to induce customers to buy, its salespeople to call on willing customers, and its HR managers to hire the right types of people, all these objectives can be achieved with the help of AI.

Making the Kroger Co. more efficient and effective

The Kroger Co. and its subsidiary 84.51° for data science, insights, and media provide an example of this strategy execution. In 2017, the giant grocery chain announced its "Restock Kroger" strategy, which better positioned the company to compete effectively in an evolving business environment. Two of the four major components of the strategy were heavily dependent on analytics and AI. In an article describing the strategy, data, analytics, personalization through AI, and the 84.51° organization were heavily featured, particularly in the first objective:

> ***Redefine the Food and Grocery Customer Experience:***
> Kroger will "accelerate" digital and ecommerce activity, "applying its customer data and personalization expertise through (in-house agency) 84.51° to even more aspects of the business, and building on the outstanding growth of the private label portfolio."
>
> - *Data & Personalization:* Using shopper data to "create different experiences for customers." Kroger already delivers more than three billion personalized recommendations annually.
>
> - *Digital:* Content goals involve providing not only functional information but also "inspiration and personalized discovery" via recipes and product-related content.
>
> - *Space Optimization:* Kroger will "leverage customer science to make space-planning decisions to disrupt shelf, optimize assortment and improve in-stocks."
>
> - *Private Label:* Kroger will "continue investing to grow its most popular brands." Sales of own brand products jumped 37 percent to $20.5 billion from 2011 to 2017.
>
> - *Smart Pricing:* The company will continue an investment to which it's devoted more than $4 billion since 2001 "to avoid losing customers because of price."[13]

Except for the private label focus, all the initiatives mentioned are data, analytics, and AI-intensive. In its second strategic platform, Expand Partnerships to Create Customer Value, there was also a mention of expanding the company's IoT sensor, video analytics, and machine learning networks, with complementary innovation through robotics and artificial intelligence to transform the customer experience.

We should note, given our previous discussion on ecosystems, that the Kroger Co. uses that term to describe the data-driven relationships it has with its consumer-packaged goods suppliers. And again, all or most of the company's strategic initiatives are dependent upon data, analytics, and AI capabilities from 84.51°. The same article that announced the new strategy mentions the group prominently, even quoting its then-leader Stuart Aitken (now chief merchant and marketing officer):

> Meanwhile, Kroger's in-house analytics and marketing firm, 84.51°, unveiled Kroger Precision Marketing, a "cross-channel media solution" that will seek to amplify the retailer's personalized communication programs.
>
> The program will leverage purchase data from Kroger's 60 million shopper households (across 2,800 stores and 35 states) to create and execute "holistic campaigns across an expanded digital ecosystem," the company said in a release. . . . "This platform fuels two parts of the Restock Kroger Plan: Redefine the Food and Grocery Customer Experience and Expand Partnerships to Create Customer Value," said 84.51° CEO Stuart Aitken. "Enhancing personalization and creating alternative revenue streams, as we will through this platform, are focus areas."

It is certainly an indication that data and AI are critical to a company's strategy when the unit that provides those capabilities—and several of its initiatives—is mentioned prominently in the article describing that strategy. In the presentation for the investors conference described in the article, "data and science drive the model" is perhaps the most prominent theme, with the elaboration of "seeing customers through data."[14]

In 2021, the Kroger Co. announced its new strategy, called "Leading with Fresh and Accelerating with Digital."[15] It again mentioned its personalization of customer offers as a "competitive moat" in its investor presentation, and said it had delivered eleven billion personalized recommendations per week in 2020—an impossible task without AI. In digital fulfillment, the company also announced the opening of its first robotics-based customer fulfillment center with UK vendor Ocado, which is the first of twenty to be built. Ocado partners with several retailers around the world, but it has an exclusive partnership with the Kroger Co. in the United States, which made a minority investment in the company. Ocado says that it uses a variety of AI programs, including:

- Twenty million demand forecasts a day to reduce out-of-stock items and food waste

- Predicting when food should arrive at the distribution center for optimal freshness

- Spotting food close to expiration dates for discounting or donation

- A hyperpersonalized digital ordering experience

- An AI-based "air traffic control system" for robots in the warehouse

- Computer vision and planning system for bag-packing robots

- Optimization of delivery vehicle loads and times.[16]

The Kroger Co. clearly depends on AI for the execution of its business strategies. Some of those strategies are impossible without AI; others are made better, cheaper, or faster with AI. While the retailer's primary focus is on doing its existing business better with AI, it is also using the technology and its data to enter new businesses (such as Kroger Precision Marketing) and to drive new ecosystems.

Strategy Archetype 3:
Influencing Customer Behavior

One of the newest strategic objectives for AI is influencing customer behavior. This archetype may have gathered attention with the astounding commercial and behavioral impact of AI in companies like Google, Facebook, TikTok, and other social media providers. They have been enormously successful in changing purchasing, socializing, information consumption, information sharing, and other behaviors of their customers—some intended and some not. The intended behaviors have made the companies enormously successful and fast-growing from a financial standpoint. The unintended behaviors, including political and social polarization, sharing of misinformation, distraction, cyberbullying, insecurity, depression, and so on, have received attention from many observers, including legislators. The AI algorithms used by these companies are intimately involved in both the positive and negative behaviors in their customers, as described by numerous researchers.[17]

Our focus is not on these digital native companies, nor on the positive or negative behaviors they induce in their customers. However, other types of companies have noticed that digital platforms, detailed data, and AI algorithms can change other types of behaviors. For the most part it's still early days for this approach, but both legacy companies and startups are attempting to change behavior with AI.

To be fair, this approach of influencing behavior isn't really new. It was pioneered by Fair, Isaac & Co. (now FICO), which created the first credit score in 1958. Takeup was slow, however, and the first behavior scoring system for a credit provider was developed for Wells Fargo in 1975. The credit score was one of the first commercial applications of machine learning. It used statistical analysis of borrowing and payment data to determine what factors were correlated with paying loans back, then used the resulting model to score each consumer with a credit history.

The metric that FICO was attempting to monitor and improve in consumers was financial responsibility—a compilation of behaviors including paying bills on time, not taking on too many credit cards, not maintaining high payment balances, and the like. FICO has done an excellent job not only of computing credit scores for hundreds of millions of people, but also persuading financial services organizations to adopt the scores for their lending decisions, as well as communicating to credit score holders how their scores are calculated and how to improve them.

Credit scores created by machine learning have now been joined by various other types of scores. Progressive Insurance, whose AI activities we will describe further in chapter 6, computes a driving score based on telematics data from its Snapshot program (though it converts the score into letter grades for consumers).[18] FICO now offers a safe driving score as well. We've discussed Lark's partnership with Anthem in this chapter, and that company computes a variety of scores for health conditions. We'll describe another example at a startup called Well in chapter 7 involving the creation of various health condition scores, as well as a score summarizing adherence to prescribed medical interventions. Manulife and its subsidiary John Hancock, and a variety of other life insurers around the world, use machine learning to monitor and to try to change health behaviors to help customers be healthier. All of these (except for credit scores) are in the relatively early stages, but they show potential to improve the relevant behaviors. Because they rely on both voluminous data and a scoring process for each customer, they wouldn't be possible without machine learning.

The Process for Strategic AI

If AI is going to enable new strategies, business models, and customer behaviors, it doesn't make sense to manage the technology bottom-up. Transformative, critically important resources like AI are by definition strategic for these organizations and should be the focus of both senior executives and strategy groups as to how they will be used in the business. Strategists should assist in decisions about priorities for AI use cases and implications for products, processes, and relationships within the company.

AI and strategy should be connected in two major ways. The first, as we've discussed in this chapter, is how AI affects or enables business strategy. If it can improve products and services, augment business models, transform channels to customers, optimize supply chains, and so forth, it should be part of a company's strategic deliberations.

The second strategic focus is to develop a strategy for AI itself. Many key decisions must be made about how a company uses and manages AI, including how it builds or buys AI capability, where it sources key talent, what projects it takes on, and how AI initiatives relate to digital platforms and processes. All these decisions both shape strategy and are shaped by it, so they should be discussed at a strategic level.

The Deloitte 2021 "State of AI in the Enterprise" survey suggests that certain aspects of strategy are typical of AI leaders. Those survey participants who were furthest along with AI were more likely to agree that they have an AI strategy, that their AI usage differentiated them from their competitors, that their senior leaders articulated a vision for how AI will change operations, and that their AI initiatives are important to their remaining competitive over the next five years (figure 3-1).

For strategic decisions to be influenced by AI in the appropriate fashion, a few preconditions apply:

- Educating senior managers on AI is critical. For a strategy process to incorporate AI, senior managers who participate in strategic planning need some familiarity with the different AI technologies and use cases for which they are appropriate.

FIGURE 3-1

Leading AI strategy practices

Percentage of respondents who selected "completely agree" or "very important" to these statements about strategy

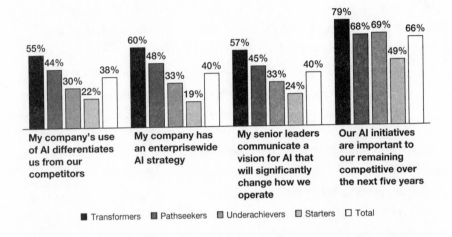

Source: Deloitte Insights, "2021 State of AI in the Enterprise," Survey Report, 4th Edition, https://www2 .deloitte.com/content/dam/insights/articles/US144384_CIR-State-of-AI-4th-edition/DI_CIR-State-of-AI -4th-edition.pdf.

AI-focused strategy is a "matching" process of business initiatives and AI capabilities, and participants need an awareness of both. The strategy function or an AI center of excellence may want to sponsor formal or informal education initiatives to ensure broad engagement and participation in the AI-related aspects of business strategy.

- Within the strategic process, the enabling effect of AI and other technologies needs to be incorporated into the consideration of strategic alternatives. This may require changes to the methodology for strategic planning. For example, a company might ask, "What could we accomplish in our marketing programs if we had better predictions of customer behavior using machine learning? How could we transform customer service with a conversational agent?" There can't be AI-rich strategic initiatives without an ideation process that includes AI capabilities.

- Beyond ideation, AI will only be embedded into a company's products and processes if it actually deploys the systems that perform the needed AI tasks. Creating linkages between a strategy and the AI development/deployment cycle is critical for getting strategic AI systems in place. Strategists will need influence the prioritization of AI projects and should have the ability to monitor AI project progress.

In this chapter we've considered five different linkages between AI and strategy—with new strategies and markets, new products and services, new business models and ecosystems, new customer behaviors, and operational strategy execution. Some large organizations, like Ping An, the Kroger Co. and Anthem, Inc., may actually take on three or four different archetypes. But the important thing in AI-powered organizations is that AI does something substantial to improve the performance or growth of the organization. Otherwise, it would be difficult to say that AI is really making a difference. And while AI and its related technologies can help with the improvement, they can sometimes be an obstacle to it. That's the subject of chapter 4.

CHAPTER 4

Technology and Data

Note that we have described the organizational and leadership aspects of AI-focused organizations before any significant mention of technology. The human aspects of AI are the most differentiating and critical, and often the most challenging. However, a company doesn't accomplish great things in AI without making extensive use of AI technologies, and virtually nothing can be done without substantial amounts of data. That's true of every all-in on AI company we have identified, and we'll describe their technology environments in this chapter.

It's never a great idea to adopt technology for its own sake, but the AI-fueled organizations we'll describe have clear business objectives for their AI technology initiatives. They include:

- Supporting a broad range of AI use cases by creating a broad AI toolkit

- Building applications faster and better with tools like automated machine learning

- Achieving a broad scale of AI deployment

- Managing and improving data for model training and other purposes

- Dealing with legacy applications and complex technology architectures

- Building or sourcing a high-performance computing infrastructure for AI

- Improving IT operations with AI

We will illustrate each of these objectives with a particular example of an AI-focused company that has pursued it and describe the technologies they adopted to do so.

Using All the Tools in the Toolkit

Companies that compete on AI realize that there are many different AI technologies, and they are usually willing to make use of all of them. Different technologies are useful for different use cases, and organizations that adopt AI broadly and deeply have breadth in their use cases and the technologies that are applied to them. DBS Bank, for example, uses a wide range of technologies across its roughly 150 different AI projects.

Financial crime prevention is important for any bank, and DBS has invested in advanced analytics and machine learning to make it better. Rule-based systems are often considered obsolete, but they are common in fraud and anti–money laundering systems, and DBS uses them for that purpose. One of their common shortcomings, however, is that they create far too many false positives—as many as 98 percent at DBS. So the bank's Transaction Surveillance group created a machine learning model that uses more of the bank's data and prioritizes the list of suspicious cases. Each case is given a risk score, and the lowest risk cases are put into hibernation and monitored for changes in risk patterns. The Transaction Surveillance group also developed a network link analysis capability using a graph database to analyze relationships among potential fraudsters and machine learning to detect suspicious networks, as well as a new data flow platform for the organization using open-source technologies.

DBS uses machine learning of various types—neural networks for credit decision-making, deep learning models for image and speech recognition, and traditional machine learning models for predicting attrition and cash outages in automated teller machines. Deep learning algorithms aren't widely accepted by banking regulators for credit models, but DBS is working with regulators to try to apply their precision to bank decisions.

All these AI technologies at DBS require supporting infrastructures, and DBS has invested in many of them. The bank transformed its data architecture and created a new data platform called ADA—Advancing DBS with AI. It includes a variety of capabilities for data ingestion, security, storage, governance, visualization, and AI/analytics model management. The goal was to enable as much self-service as possible in creating new AI models and maintaining them over time. DBS has also migrated many of its AI and analytics systems to hybrid clouds to enable faster processing.

Of course, different organizations that focus on AI will need different technologies to build their use cases and accomplish their business objectives. But a large company is unlikely to get by with a single AI method or technology.

Building AI Applications Faster and Better

If your organization has embraced AI as key to its future, you'd probably like things to move a bit faster. Specifically, you'd like new AI algorithms to be developed more quickly by more data scientists.

You're in luck, because technology is making it increasingly possible for data scientists—both professional and amateur—to build new models that do an excellent job of machine learning, or predicting the future based on past data.

Machine learning, if you're not familiar with the underlying approach to it, does exactly that. Supervised learning, which is, as we've noted, the most common type of machine learning in business, trains a model using most of the data from a training data set, tests the model with the remainder of the data from that data set, and then uses the resulting model to make predictions or classifications on additional data that was not part of the training data set and where the outcome is not known. Well-developed models typically do a great job of prediction, but they can be labor-intensive to develop and deploy. To do it well typically involves feature engineering, or testing a wide variety of different versions of features or variables. It also requires time for interpreting different models, and the time to write code or APIs (application programming interfaces) to deploy and integrate the model with other systems. Unsupervised learning, which is typically used to cluster similar cases with no outcome variable, is less common in business but is beginning to grow in popularity.

All these steps, however, can now be performed with automated machine learning, or AutoML. (Even unsupervised learning has AutoML versions.) Using AutoML, the 84.51° subsidiary of the Kroger Co. is developing a "machine learning machine" that can build and deploy very large numbers of models with relatively little human intervention. The website of 84.51° provides a few revealing numerical facts that convey the enormous size and scope of their data science efforts on behalf of its retailer parent and its ecosystem partners:

- More than 1,500 consumer packaged goods companies, agencies, publishers, and business-affiliated partners

- Nearly 1 of 2 households in the United States

- 1.9 billion personalized offers delivered in 2021

- Leverages 35+ petabytes of first-party shopper data and over 2 billion annual transactions

- 2 billion customer shopping baskets analyzed

In chapter 3 we described how much the Kroger Co. depends on these efforts to fuel its strategic initiatives. The breadth and depth of data science at 84.51° also reveals how important it is for the company to employ the best possible AI technology, tools, and methods.

The current approach to machine learning at 84.51° emerged from an initiative called *embedded machine learning* (EML). Scott Crawford, a data science manager, led the initiative beginning in 2015. Milen Mahadevan, the group's current president, is a champion for the automation of processes and products within the organization. Embedding machine learning and making extensive use of AutoML is the logical progression from ad hoc modeling and segmentation to automated processes that generate value through efficiency and improved accuracy. 84.51° adopted AutoML tools and processes but did so within a broader context of a redesigned process and culture of machine learning.

AutoML provided a variety of potential benefits to the business's machine learning capabilities. Machine learning at 84.51°, unlike at many organizations, is not a static process based on a single training dataset and a model based on it. Instead, models are retrained often based on new data. For example, sales forecasting, which drives the process of ordering goods and managing inventory, evolves its model on a nightly basis based on the most recent data. Paul Helman, then the chief science officer at 84.51°, and his team developed this approach involving adaptive estimators because they realized it was important for efficiently modeling complex and changing human behaviors such as shopping preferences.

EML eventually became a formal mission not just to adopt AutoML, but more broadly to enable, empower, and engage the organization to better use and embed machine learning. "Enable" meant providing the infrastructure—such as the servers, software, and data connectivity—to efficiently use and embed machine learning. "Empower" involved identification of the best set of machine learning tools and training analysts, and the data scientists to use those tools. After evaluating more than fifty tools, 84.51° selected R, Python, and Julia as its preferred machine learning languages, and DataRobot (a Deloitte collaborator, and a company that Tom advises) as its primary AutoML software provider. "Engage" meant motivating internal clients to use the tools by demonstrating and socializing the benefits through several proofs of concept, advancing code sharing/ examples (via Github, a code repository to facilitate sharing), and consulting.

Another part of the EML initiative was to develop a standard methodology for machine learning use. Its internally developed methodology, which it calls "8PML" (84.51° Process for Machine Learning), is unusual within nonvendor organizations. Scott Crawford says that it borrows heavily from several publicly available data mining processes but was customized to better fit 84.51°-specific use cases and environments. It has three major components: solution engineering, model development, and model deployment.

Solution engineering

After the necessary training data has been gathered, most machine learning efforts in companies are focused on the development of models, but 84.51° was interested in a broader focus. Its leaders realized that models that aren't deployed provide no economic value, and analytical problems that are framed incorrectly can do more harm than good. The 8PML begins with the solution engineering phase, in which the analysis is framed, and the business objectives for the project are clarified and compared to available resources. For example, a project's business objective might require a very large number of models to be routinely updated and quickly deployed, without the requisite budget and staffing. In the past, solution engineering would require rethinking the problem to stay within resource constraints. Automated machine learning technology can substantially lessen those resource constraints. Solution engineering is still necessary, but the horizon of solutions has broadened.

Model development

In the model development phase of the methodology, data is analyzed, variables or features are engineered, and the model that best fits the training data is identified. AutoML using DataRobot speeds this phase of the process considerably, increasing the productivity of data scientists. That frees them up to fit more models and/or to give more effort to other high-value aspects of the process (e.g., solution engineering, feature engineering, and so forth). The technology also makes it possible for less skilled practitioners of data science to generate high-quality models. Detailed knowledge of which algorithms are appropriate for certain analyses is no longer essential; automated machine learning takes over that function.

Because matching algorithms to problems was previously the job of professional data scientists, it's not uncommon for them to distrust AutoML or to believe that it can't create effective models. At 84.51°, some experienced data scientists were initially concerned that they would be moving to a world in which their deep and hard-earned knowledge of algorithms and methods would have no currency. The company's leaders emphasized that the new tools would empower people to do their work more efficiently. Over time, this proved to be the case, and now there is little or no pushback from the experienced data scientists about the use of the DataRobot tool.

The initial focus for AutoML at 84.51° was to improve the productivity of professional data scientists. But the unit has also used the automated tools to expand the number of people who can use and apply machine learning. 84.51° has been growing its data science function to meet the rapidly expanding demand for modeling and analytics to solve complex business problems. It is a challenge at any company to find well-trained data scientists, so 84.51° employs AutoML to make it possible for those without traditional data science training to create machine learning models. 84.51° now regularly hires "insights specialists"—people who don't have as much experience with machine learning, but who are skilled at communicating and presenting results, and who have high business acumen. Aided by AutoML, a substantial number of activities within traditional model development such as use case identification and exploratory analyses can now also be done by these insights specialists. The data scientists with more statistical and machine learning experience can focus their time on the aspects of machine learning that require their deeper expertise, and also spend more time training and consulting with others who have less experience.

Model deployment

The third and final component of the 84.51° approach to machine learning is model deployment, in which the chosen model is deployed in production systems and processes. Given the scale of machine learning applications at the Kroger Co.—the sales forecasting application, for example, creates forecasts for each item in each of more than 2,500 stores for each of the subsequent fourteen days—this stage of the process is key. And as Scott Crawford points out, issues around deployment (or "productionalization," as he refers to it) are often underestimated:

> Prior to my current role facilitating the use of machine learning at 84.51°, my work experiences included building and deploying models at one of the nation's largest insurance companies and one of the world's largest banks. One commonality across all

my experiences is that productionalization is often the most
challenging phase of machine learning projects. The require-
ment of a production deployment often severely constrains
the viable solutions. For example, productionalization might
require code to be delivered in a specific language (e.g., C++,
SQL, Java) and/or to meet strict latency thresholds.

Automated machine learning tools can help with the deployment
process by generating code or APIs that embed the model. For example, 84.51° often makes use of DataRobot's ability to output Java
code for data preprocessing and model scoring.

Many companies today are experimenting with AutoML and
related tools, but 84.51° and the Kroger Co. have taken this AI
approach to the next level. The embedded machine learning initiative, standardizing on an automated machine learning tool, and the
three-stage machine learning methodology have all helped to create
a machine learning machine. Models are framed, developed, and
deployed in the same way that a well-managed manufacturing organization might create physical products. We'll probably see multiple
examples of this factory-like approach to machine learning in the
future, but 84.51° is practicing it today.

Getting to Scale

One of the key challenges for many organizations with AI is getting
to a sufficient scale to make a difference in their operations and
performance. Technology can help companies achieve this objective,
though as with the other AI objectives we have described the complete answer is to combine technology with other changes like new
processes and newly involved groups of people.

Our 2021 survey addressed this issue of scaled AI operations in
multiple questions. High-achieving organizations with AI, labeled

transformers and pathseekers, were more likely (typically by about 25 percent) than the two lower-achieving groups (starters and under-achievers) to agree that they have adopted several different AI oper-ational practices that facilitate scaling and ongoing management of AI. They include a documented process or life cycle for AI models; the use of machine learning operations (or MLOps) to manage models in production and ensure their ongoing effectiveness; new team struc-tures and workflows to manage AI; and new job roles (including prod-uct managers, data engineers, and machine learning engineers) to maximize AI advancements (figure 4-1).

Shell is an example of both the need for AI scale and the ability to achieve it rapidly. The company is pursuing several different business objectives with AI: improving their understanding of the

FIGURE 4-1

Leading AI operations practices

Percentage of respondents who selected "completely agree" to these statements about operations

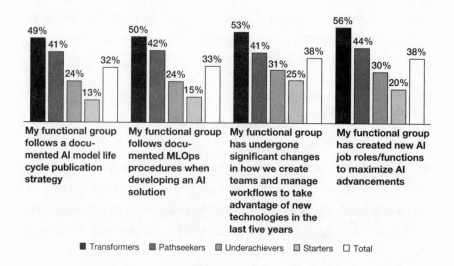

Source: Deloitte Insights, "2021 State of AI in the Enterprise," Survey Report, 4th Edition, https://www2 .deloitte.com/content/dam/insights/articles/US144384_CIR-State-of-AI-4th-edition/DI_CIR-State-of-AI -4th-edition.pdf.

subsurface more rapidly, maximizing recovery of new and existing fields, making their existing asset operations more effective and energy efficient, and offering low carbon solutions to customers—for example, by optimizing electric vehicle charging and integrating renewable energy into electricity systems.

The maintenance process in particular requires significant scale in order to have impact, as Shell has hundreds of thousands of pieces of equipment requiring maintenance across all its facilities. Dan Jeavons, who heads digital innovation and computational science for Shell, has had to employ a variety of technologies and approaches to achieve scale in that domain. One approach is to use predictive maintenance—a technique for predicting when equipment will degrade in performance or break down, rather than maintaining it at standard intervals or waiting for it to break down. Shell executives are convinced that predictive maintenance can make equipment more reliable and maintenance more efficient, as well as helping to improve process safety.

Jeavons felt that the AI needs for predictive maintenance models— they generally employ supervised machine learning on each component that requires monitoring—were greater than any centralized group of data scientists could handle. So Shell decided to recruit and train the engineers who already worked with the plant and equipment in AI techniques so that they could develop, interpret, and maintain predictive maintenance models over time on a self-service basis.

Over five thousand people (from an inner core of thirty people in 2013) are in the outer core of the AI community at Shell now, with more on the way. Many of them are engineers who create and oversee predictive maintenance models. Shell partnered with Udacity to create online training in AI methods and techniques. Data from equipment like compressors, instruments, pumps, and control valves is aggregated into a central data platform, with "1.9 trillion rows of data" thus far, according to Jeavons. Shell has partnered with

Microsoft for use of its cloud service Azure to process the data, and it's stored with Databricks' data lake software called Delta Lake.

Engineers can now use custom built AutoML tools to generate models, and they have been trained in the skills to validate the selected models. They can also maintain the models over time after they are in production and ensure that they still predict well using an MLOps tool. Jeavons describes it as the "one of the world's largest" MLOps applications in the industrial domain. Both are part of the ecosystem we described in chapter 3 that Shell has developed with C3.AI and Baker Hughes.

Over ten thousand pieces of equipment are monitored every day and their data evaluated with AI-based predictive maintenance models, and this number is increasing by several hundred pieces of equipment each week. Jeavons said that the engineers doing this work tend to enjoy the process of learning about machine learning, and since they know the equipment, they are well suited to interpreting and acting on the models.

Given the diverse range of people at Shell who develop and maintain models and the goal of sharing assets around the company, it was important for them to use similar processes for AI and system development. Shell partnered with Microsoft to make development tools and methods available; they included DevOps (a methodology and toolset for integrating development, IT operations, quality management, and cybersecurity), Azure Boards (dashboards for planning, tracking, and discussing development work across teams), Azure Pipelines (a set of tools and processes for automating system development and deployment) and Github. The widespread use of these tools has enabled Shell to share code and algorithms, and deploy them rapidly and successfully.

In areas outside of predictive maintenance, Shell has employed some of these same approaches—expanding participation in AI, using common processes, and partnering with external providers. It also uses additional technologies. In pipeline maintenance, for example, Shell is employing cameras on drones to take photographs of pipes and then using deep learning models to detect potential maintenance issues. The accuracy of the AI image recognition is close to that of human inspectors, and the time it takes to inspect is much less. At some Shell facilities, it took six years to inspect all piping; the drone and the AI system can do it in a few days. Human inspectors (sometimes at remote sites) can then confirm and prioritize the judgments made by the deep learning image recognition models. Facilities need a smaller number of onsite inspectors, who do more advanced verification. The inspectors needed some convincing to believe in the accuracy of the drone/AI approach and to adopt the new process, but they are now on board.

Shell is also pursuing AI-enabled changes in the process of subsurface exploration. Shell realized that its subsurface data was located across multiple silos and not easily accessible for analysis, so it created a subsurface data universe. But Shell executives quickly realized that its many collaborators in subsurface exploration needed access to the data as well.

Shell and its business partners created an approach we discussed in chapter 3 with reference to Shell and others—a data and algorithm-sharing ecosystem. The Open Subsurface Data Universe (OSDU) ecosystem is only a few years old but already quite large; it consists of over 160 companies, including energy companies, technology vendors, consultants, and academic researchers. Its primary focus is the exchange of data across organizations, but it is also a vehicle to share models, applications, platforms, and training materials. The ecosystem shares seismic, well, reservoir, and production data, and there are standards for each type.

Other AI-fueled organizations have different approaches to scaling AI based on their circumstances, and they aren't all driven by technology. At Unilever, for example, the greatest challenge is scaling AI use cases across the more than one hundred countries in which the company does business. As it rolls out new capabilities for advanced analytics and AI in the areas of supply chain, precision marketing, pricing, and promotions, it works with leaders in each country (at least those in large markets) to customize its models and integrate them with local systems and processes.

In India, for example, Hindustan Unilever sells its products into nine out of ten households, but many consumers buy their products from small local grocery stores—millions of them across the country. Historically, product assortments were based on what Unilever had shipped to the store in the past. But now Unilever's data scientists have developed thousands of models to customize store assortments based on past sales, consumption patterns in the local area, living standards near the store, and product categories experiencing growth, even from competitors.

These models and level of granularity work well for India, but the approach to countries that shop in large grocery chains (Kroger Co. in the United States for example), shopping clubs (Costco and Sam's Club in the United States), hypermarkets (Carrefour in France), or convenience stores (7-11 in Japan) need to be very different. Andy Hill, who heads data, analytics, and AI for Unilever, told us that "scaling for us is a matter not of developing models, but of change management and deployment across the globe."

Managing Data for Training and Everything Else

Data is the precursor of machine learning success, and models can't achieve accurate predictions without large quantities of good data. Every organization that's serious about AI must deal with its data at some point—structuring or rearchitecting it, putting it on a common platform, and addressing pesky issues like data quality, duplicated data, and siloed data throughout the company. It's fair to say that the single biggest obstacle for most organizations in scaling AI systems is acquiring, cleaning, and integrating the right data.

We've already described several major data initiatives: Piyush Gupta's involvement in DBS Bank's data redesign in chapter 2, as well as the Advancing DBS with AI data project and Shell's vast collection of predictive maintenance data described earlier in this chapter. We could say similar things about Unilever. That company has also been working on a new cloud-based data platform for analytics and AI. Like Shell, they are employing a lakehouse architecture that combines a data lake for unstructured data and some traditional relational data for business intelligence applications. It is the "single source of truth" for company data and gives Unilever the ability to scale the repository easily and handle intensive analytics and AI workloads.

Data environments for AI-oriented companies have several characteristics:

- *Most are cloud-based.* They provide easy access, the flexibility to scale to more computing power, and multiple AI application software tools. Some aggressive users of AI, such as Capital One, claim that because they need to devote less time and attention to data storage and infrastructure management since moving to the cloud, they are able to significantly grow their AI focus and capabilities. If for some reason an organization needs on-premise computing and storage (e.g., for security, latency, or regulatory purposes), the same AI technologies are available in that context.

- *The data they use is machine readable.* It typically requires some extraction, classification, and preparation, but data needs to be structured—typically in rows and columns of numbers, or at least in categorized text fields—to be AI ready. Key data needs to be extracted from formats like faxes, handwritten notes, speech recordings, images, and videos for companies to extract deeper insights from their data.

- *They involve internal and external data.* Companies are analyzing geospatial, social media, weather, image, and other types of external data, and comparing it to their own internal transaction data. The internal data can be stored and analyzed in the traditional row and column format, while external data can be stored in whatever form it was created in. Even unstructured data types eventually need to be transformed into rows and columns of numbers for analysis, however.

- *They are centralized.* Most of the AI-first companies we spoke with are attempting to get away from the many data silos their organization previously maintained, and move to one data platform for virtually all data that's used by analytics or AI. There is a move in some organizations to shift to a data mesh or data fabric environment that integrates data from multiple sources around the organization, but this is in its early stages.

- *They have a different focus.* For purposes of AI and analytics, companies are emphasizing some of the latter steps in the data supply chain that involve consumption, rather than the focus on data capture, collection, and storage that they previously emphasized.[1] Many are also emphasizing the creation of data products for internal or customer use that combine data and analytical or AI models in one offering.

- *They use new systems.* Companies that need data for AI are also increasingly finding that they need AI for data. They are using, for example, probabilistic matching machine learning systems to combine data about the same product, customer, or supplier across different databases. AI systems are also

aiding somewhat in data preparation, pointing out data
quality problems and suggesting approaches to resolving
them. AI systems can also create automated data catalogs,
which help users of the data find what they need. Juan Tello,
Deloitte Consulting LLP's chief data officer, also points out
that AI can help organizations comply with regulations such
as the European GDPR and California's CCPA. It can help
determine where privacy violations might occur and, in some
cases, resolve them.[2]

- *They are adding team members.* Despite some help from
  AI, wrangling data is still a labor-intensive activity. Many
  companies, therefore, are now including data engineers on
  AI teams. Their role is to build high-quality, high-volume
  data environments that make it possible to train AI models
  and apply them to production data. Performing these tasks
  frees data scientists to focus more on algorithm development
  and feature engineering, and speeds up system deployment.

There is no doubt that data platforms will continue to be one of
the most important prerequisites for successful AI. But the rise of
the approaches we've described has the potential to make data management for AI significantly more efficient and effective.

The Burden of Legacy Applications and Architectures and How to Deal with Them

One important, if less than exciting, issue of technology for AI is how
to deal with legacy transaction applications and complex existing
technology architectures. AI systems that make predictions or recommendations, or those that facilitate user interactions with computer systems, need to integrate with transactional systems if they
are going to be fully deployed. Many companies have old, fragmented

legacy systems, which makes integration challenging. In many cases, they need to modernize these systems in order to integrate AI capabilities with them.

Large legacy organizations also have complex AI architectures with complex technology stacks. This is particularly true in companies with substantial entrepreneurial AI activity across the organization and no strong central coordination. Many of the resulting AI technologies overlap with each other's capabilities. Leaders struggle to even know who uses what in their organizations and how to unify and manage it all. Companies in this situation typically have multiple cloud systems, multiple AI development tools, and many alliances, which all becomes unwieldy and suboptimal. Companies in this situation have to get control of these diverse architectures and simplify them over time.

The health benefits company Anthem Inc. is a useful example, in part because it illustrates the sobering nature of the task. We first began to study and consult on this issue at Anthem several years ago. Tom Miller, then Anthem's CIO, spoke at a Deloitte conference in 2017. Deloitte was working closely with Anthem at the time to help make the company AI first. Miller described how the company was managing its legacy systems.

He said that the core of Anthem's transactional architecture was (and still is) its claims engine, which processes over a billion claims a year. In 2017 Anthem was modernizing its claims engine to combine multiple systems (several came into the company through acquisitions) into a single platform, making key services modular (enrollment, billing, pricing, and so forth), and integrating AI capabilities into the core system and process. The goal was to include such cognitive capabilities as machine learning insights, conversational AI at the customer interface, and robotic process automation. The company created a cognitive capability office for just that purpose.

As Anthem has continued its modernization efforts, they have been consolidating their claims processing into one core system, transitioning into a cloud platform with APIs. This cloud platform will drive interoperability across systems, enhance their ability to increase efficiency, and drive cost savings through AI. These changes are well underway, but the organization's architectural approaches have evolved somewhat. Rajeev Ronanki, our former Deloitte colleague who became Anthem's chief digital officer in 2018 and is now the president of their platform business, said that much of the AI functionality at Anthem will be provided through APIs rather than building it into the code of transactional systems. Changes in their technology environment are incorporated into a series of three-year plans.

In the next three-year plan, Anthem has ambitious technology goals. Automation will be a major focus, with a goal of automating 50 percent of the company's work tasks. The goal of the next plan is also to have 90 percent of interactions with stakeholders to be digital and AI-based.

We think that Anthem's three-year plans are a good way to transition a legacy architecture to one based on AI. Any legacy company with technical debt accumulated over time can't afford to rebuild everything at once. Even if they could, with the pace of change in AI it would probably be somewhat obsolete by the time the new technology architecture was built. The key is to set clear goals and show clear value at each step along the way of a multi-year plan for change.

AI, Digital, and AIOps

One of the most popular applications for AI in recent years, according to Deloitte's annual survey of AI activity, is IT itself. AI and automation capabilities can predict and diagnose problems in networks and servers, and automation programs can restore them to health. This sort of AI use case may seem a bit inwardly focused, but it has actually become a critical capability for many organizations. If your business depends on IT and digital capabilities, you need to harness all the tools at your disposal to ensure the availability of those resources.

The use of AI to help with IT operations has been called *IT autonomics*, but more recently goes by the term *AIOps*. AIOps involves software and IT device data to identify problem areas and automate aspects of IT operations. The technology hasn't replaced human IT operators as companies have become increasingly digitized, but it has helped to limit the growth of this type of job to a reasonable level.

One AI-focused company that has embraced AIOps is Airbus. It has hundreds of thousands of IT devices, and they are increasingly integral to the production of airplanes and other products. If critical IT equipment goes down, or if there aren't spares immediately available, production may be interrupted. The company is using AI to predict and prevent outages of IT equipment, and to shorten the time to repair them. Airbus is also using AIOps to monitor the delivery of information to the Skywise open data platform that we described in chapter 3.

Airbus has partnered with the software company Splunk to monitor and control many different machines in its production process, as well as its cybersecurity environment. Over eighteen months Airbus developed a global data fusion platform that monitors twenty terabytes of data a day from 200,000 data-generating assets. The monitoring system has over 120 different applications, many of which have machine learning capabilities. They assess such issues as whether IT assets are operating at optimal levels, what spare components might be available if something goes wrong, and the potential for internal or external data breach or insider security threats. There's no way that any company could keep track of and successfully manage all that data and applications without help from AI.

Airbus isn't unique. It's clear that companies with a substantial digital presence should ensure that their end-to-end IT and digital infrastructure is available all the time, or as much as possible. AI-powered companies are also digitally powered, and they need AIOps to keep the digital fuel flowing.

Building High-Performance Computing Environments

AI technology isn't only about software. Companies that plan to do significant amounts of AI development need to establish a suitable hardware environment. Often called *high-performance computing* or HPC environments, they typically include systems that can perform very fast numeric calculations in parallel. Most commonly, deep learning-based AI models use graphics processing units (GPUs) that are available in both cloud and on-premise configurations. Originally developed for video games, they are particularly well suited for image, video, and natural language processing. Companies also need considerable storage for the extensive data required to train machine learning models, and may require low-latency architectures for real-time scoring of models. Other types of AI methods require powerful versions of regular processors.

Deloitte, for example, stood up the Deloitte Center for AI Computing in collaboration with Nvidia, which supplied its GPU-enabled DGX A100 system, to prove out new use cases, co-innovate with clients, and capture growth by creating and selling new products and services using this advanced AI infrastructure.

The Pace of Change in AI Technology

AI technology is perhaps the fastest changing of any information technology domain. Thousands of researchers are exploring new models and AI approaches, and thousands of established vendors are

attempting to turn them into products. Particular vendors, specifically startups, wax and wane over time. No organization should
expect that they can establish a technology environment for AI and
let it ride for a decade. Constant monitoring of external offerings and
their match (or mismatch) to internal needs is critical in the AI space.

We believe that every large organization—and certainly those that
are or aspire to be AI first—should designate smart people to follow
AI technology trends, try out new technologies, and import them
when they seem to fit the organization's needs. These people don't
need to be fantastic data scientists or AI engineers, but they do need
to understand the key technologies in AI and how they support use
cases and business needs.

One final note: in virtually every discussion in this chapter about
the technology that companies use to advance their AI, we also discussed other types of organizational changes they made—that old
triumvirate of people, process, and technology, to which we might
add strategy and business model changes. AI technology is powerful stuff, but it isn't useful without changes in the business, the
organization, and its culture.

CHAPTER 5

Capabilities

The old management cliché about any type of major business change—"X is a journey"—applies to AI-enabled business transformations. No company adopts AI extensively and deeply at once. It takes experimentation, development of capability over time, fits and starts, mistakes and setbacks, and all the other attributes of any major change within an organization. What matters is how companies build sustainable AI capabilities over time.

In this chapter we'll describe those capabilities and how they are built. We'll describe some companies' specific journeys to achieve the AI archetypes to which they aspire, as well as some general principles of moving up the AI capability ladder. We'll point out some shortcuts that organizations may want to adopt. We'll also mention some pitfalls that some organizations have encountered in their AI initiatives that you may want to avoid. We'll conclude the chapter by discussing ethical, trustworthy AI capabilities and how they can be put into place.

The General Path to Being AI Fueled

The path to becoming all-in on AI is not particularly well trodden; we've estimated that fewer than 1 percent of large organizations would meet our definition of the term. However, there are capability maturity models for virtually every business capability, and we will describe a similar approach for AI. Advancing maturity in AI is based on a variety of factors, including:

- Breadth of AI use cases across the enterprise

- Breadth of different AI technologies employed

- Level of engagement by senior leaders

- The role of data in enterprise decision-making

- Extent of AI resources available—data, people, technology

- Extent of production deployments, as opposed to AI pilots or experiments

- Links to transformation of business strategy or business models

- Policies and processes to ensure ethical use of AI

Capability maturity models tend to have five levels, and we see no reason to depart from that standard. They also tend to have low capabilities at Level 1 and high ones at Level 5, and we follow that pattern as well. The levels of capabilities that we presented in chapter 1 are repeated here with levels:

- *AI fueled (Level 5)*. Have all or most of the components we've described above, fully implemented and functioning—the business is built on AI capabilities and is becoming a learning machine (see the next section);

- *Transformers (Level 4).* Are not yet AI fueled but are relatively far along in the journey, with some of the attributes in place; have multiple AI deployments that are creating substantial value for the organization;

- *Pathseekers (Level 3).* Have already started on the journey and are making progress, but at an early stage—have some deployed systems and a few measurable positive outcomes achieved;

- *Starters (Level 2).* Are experimenting with AI—these companies have a plan but need to do a lot more to progress; have very few or no production deployments;

- *Underachievers (Level 1).* Have started experimenting with AI but have no production deployments and have achieved little to no economic value.

We might also add a "Level 0" to describe companies that have no AI activity whatsoever, but this is certainly a minority category among large firms in sophisticated economies. The key difference with other maturity models is that we're offering three alternative archetypes for the use of AI, but a company can be at various levels no matter what the primary focus of their efforts.

We would argue that in talking about AI-fueled enterprises, we are almost always describing Level 5 organizations. Like our examples, they are companies that have a wide variety of AI technologies and use cases in place, along with specialized technology platforms to support them. They do experiment, and companies striving to create may do more experimentation than those seeking operational improvements. The goal of all these organizations, however—usually achieved—is to actually do business with AI by putting AI systems into production deployment. New business processes are employed. New products and services are introduced to the marketplace and used by customers. Senior executives are engaged and active in identifying use cases and monitoring performance. They have established data science groups, modernized their digital infrastructures, and identified large volumes of data for training and testing models.

Perhaps most importantly, as we discussed in chapter 3, there are alternative archetypes for employing AI, and somewhat different versions of capability models for different strategies. As we noted earlier, our view is that the three major archetypes can be summarized as (1) creating new businesses, products, or services; (2) transforming operations; and (3) influencing customer behavior. While operational improvements are the most common objective for AI according to our survey research, it's clear that at least some companies don't just use AI to make their existing strategies, operations, and business models somewhat more efficient. Instead, they use it to enable new strategies, radically new business process designs, and new relationships with customers and partners. Those companies would assess their capabilities in terms of the degree to which they have successfully developed new strategies, business models, or products. Operationally focused AI objectives would involve achievement of substantial operational improvements, and customer behavior objectives would focus on how much actual customer behavior change has actually been achieved. Of course, that level of business transformation requires the active engagement and participation in strategic deliberations by senior management that Level 5 organizations typically display.

Ping An: A Clear Level 5 Firm for Creating New Business Models

It would be difficult to imagine a firm with a greater commitment to AI-fueled business than Ping An, the China-based company that started in 1988 as an insurance company. As we outlined in chapter 1, it has rapidly evolved an integrated financial services platform providing products and services in insurance, banking and investment, through lifestyle ecosystems in financial services, health-care services, auto services, and smart cities services. Ping An has used AI to create new business models, new strategies, new ecosystems, and new processes. This proved to be an excellent strategy as China's economy grew dramatically, and consumers became more affluent, in the late twentieth and early twenty-first centuries. As we discussed in chapter 3, no one could doubt that AI is being used to fuel business transformation at the company level, and that it has already done so successfully. It also, of course, uses AI to improve existing operations in its various businesses, but its primary focus is the creation of AI-fueled scenarios and business opportunities.

Ping An's senior management team is certainly engaged with AI. Peter Ma Mingzhe, the founder and chairman of the company, is closely engaged with the data science team and drives new developments in AI and related technologies. When he has an idea for a new application of AI within the business, he finds the right team to make it happen. Ma has been enthusiastic for over a decade about data, then big data, then AI. In 2013 Ma brought in Jessica Tan as chief operations and information officer. Tan came from McKinsey, the management consulting firm, and has two degrees from MIT. She's now co-CEO with Ping An's AI initiatives under her remit.

Ping An has also established a massive data science organization. As of June 2021, there were over 4,500 data scientists and AI specialists at the company, and over 110,000 scientific and technical experts. Jing Xiao, the group chief scientist and effectively head of AI, is a Carnegie Mellon PhD in computer science and robotics. Many of the company's data scientists were previously academics. The AI specialists at the company are assigned on a project basis to initiatives in particular business units. Xiao told us that the company's massive amounts of data (in part derived from its ecosystem structure) and many use cases for applying it makes it easier to attract data science talent. He also said that AI specialists don't just create models; they have responsibilities to deploy models into the business as well.

Ping An has a long inventory of AI use cases, some quite visible to the external world. In Ping An's Good Doctor platform, which helped to create a new business for the firm in health care, AI-based systems assist human doctors with symptom checking and triage, serving over four hundred million subscribers. In the Smart Cities business unit, an intelligent disease prediction system helps monitor and predict diseases like influenza and diabetes in the community of several large Chinese cities. Ping An's Auto Owner app uses AI and other digital tools to resolve car accident claims from smartphone photos in as little as two minutes. Other features of the same app can generate a recommended insurance policy for a customer in less than seven seconds. Its OneConnect business for financial services firms has a powerful AI-based risk management capability. There are many more such AI applications throughout the company.

Ping An has developed several different AI platforms to fuel these user scenario cases. Ping An Brain, for example, integrates such methods as deep learning, data mining, biological recognition, and other technologies to power scenario use cases in industrial chain event analysis, voice recognition, a recommendation engine, and robot deployments. The smart city applications like disease prediction are driven by a platform called PADIA for data-based decision-making. It incorporates a variety of AI algorithms, including machine learning and natural language processing.

Organizationally, much of Ping An's AI emanates from its Ping An Technology unit, which is based in Shenzhen, but it has labs in several other Chinese cities and elsewhere, including Singapore. Established in 2008, Ping An Technology has won numerous awards for its research projects and was ranked eighth in the world in 2019 for the number of patents it developed. Today, most of its research projects involve AI in some fashion.

Ping An has used data and scenario-based AI to fuel and transform its business from insurance more than thirty years ago to become a leading integrated financial services and health-care services provider. But there is no reason why other insurance firms—or those in other industries—couldn't adopt the same approach. Ping An has gone from a tiny company in the late 1980s to a global giant. With revenue of over $191 billion, Ping An was ranked sixteenth on the 2021 Fortune Global 500 list, and second among global financial enterprises.

Scotiabank: Slow Start, Fast Catch-Up in Operational Transformation

Some organizations and readers may feel that acquiring capabilities for AI is a race, and if a company falls behind it can never catch up. That notion is belied by Scotiabank (officially Bank of Nova Scotia), one of the "big five" banks headquartered in Canada, which has pursued a results-oriented approach to AI, accelerating its capabilities over the past two years. While some of Scotiabank's competitors built or acquired AI capabilities earlier on, Scotiabank was first focused on a large-scale digital transformation that would lay the foundation for data and analytics capabilities. While it may have slowed the bank's entry into high-end analytics and AI, this focus has enabled a highly practical, data-driven approach to responding to customer needs across the bank's various businesses.

Scotiabank has caught up in some crucial areas in AI by more closely integrating its data and analytics work; taking a pragmatic approach to AI; and focusing on reusable datasets, which help with both speed and return on investment.

By mid-2019, Brian Porter, the bank's CEO, felt it was important to get analytics right, and that a new team focused on Customer Insights, Data, and Analytics (CID&A) would be central to the task.

Porter appointed Phil Thomas as executive vice president of CID&A, with the bank's chief analytics officer and chief data officer both reporting to him. A dedicated chief information officer was added to support the function.

This integrated reporting structure allowed Scotiabank to move rapidly to gather and manage the necessary data and put analytics and AI capabilities in place. As one of the executives put it, "Our incentives, leadership, and personalities are all aligned—there is no friction or blocking."

That said, the Scotiabank executives know that success comes from the direct alignment of these elements with their business objectives. For instance, while the analytics and AI function is centralized, most of the data scientists are directly aligned to the various business lines. As a result, business leaders ultimately drive the agenda for what analytics and AI use cases are developed, partnering closely with their dedicated analytics and data teams. "Digitization has made the entire bank visible in data, and analytics and AI people are not just enablement—we are a part of the new front lines," said Grace Lee, who was chief analytics officer until October 2021. (Lee took over leadership of CID&A at that time, with Thomas moving up to chief risk officer, a role that includes oversight of CID&A.)

For Thomas, Lee, and their colleagues, improving key processes and making better decisions within the bank was the best way forward. The way they'd get there was with a results-oriented approach to AI—Thomas refers to it as "blue collar AI." The focus is not on research or experimentation, but rather on what projects have a high likelihood of delivering value to the business in a relatively short timeframe. There are no "big bang" projects, just those that involve continuous improvement of the bank's operations and customer relationships. As a result, most AI projects are deployed into production, with 80 percent of analytics and AI models already deployed and 20 percent pending, according to Lee.

Scotiabank executives recognized that dramatic changes to business models and product/service offerings could have more difficulty getting off the ground and not achieve the traction necessary to build momentum. While some resources are devoted to exploring how new technologies (not just AI, but also blockchain and quantum computing) might drive new business models and products, the great majority of the CID&A team is focused on improving operations and customer experiences today.

In keeping with the customer focus of the bank's AI approach, several of its key use cases have focused on improving customer experience. Scotiabank decided that during the Covid-19 pandemic it would try to find financial advice on how to navigate the pandemic for the customers most in need of such help (first individual consumers, and later small businesses). The team developed an application that employs a machine learning model to identify consumers who are likely to have cash flow issues using transactional data such as deposits and spending levels. With this, the bank identified those who were found to be most in need of support and advice. The CID&A team partnered with the Canadian banking retail arm of the bank to leverage these proactive contact opportunities through branch relationship managers, who would use these targeted lists to connect with customers and offer personalized advice and support.

Scotiabank also introduced an AI-driven marketing and engagement engine to support proactive interactions with customers. This engine analyzes both customer life events that the bank knows about (new mortgage, new child, child in college), and customer preferences for particular channels (branches, mobile, online, contact center, or email) to offer banking advice that's both personalized and in the channel the customer prefers.

Although the bank's primary AI focus is on customers, there are plenty of use cases in other areas as well. The bank has found substantial returns from automating tasks in the back office of its global banking and markets division, improving security on the front line, and reducing information search time in contact center responses by more than a minute per call.

The data management function at Scotiabank, headed by Peter Serenita as chief data officer, also made changes. The goal was to more rapidly provide data for analytics and AI use cases—because without the data, the models wouldn't be possible. Before the 2019 CID&A restructuring, the bank's data strategy had been primarily focused on defense—a protect-the-bank approach that emphasized regulatory compliance, financial reporting, and risk management.

With the added focus on customer insights and rapid value realization, the data function developed a new approach to data delivery that it called *reusable authoritative data set* (RAD). It identified reusable data sets for customer data, transactional data, balance data, and so forth. This approach to data enhances speed, consistency, and value. While it is typically challenging to produce high ROIs on data projects, Serenita says this is now common at Scotiabank.

Scotiabank's experience is evidence that organizations that get a slow start on AI can catch up to and even surpass competitors who started earlier, as long as these slow starters are committed to investing in and leveraging the value of AI technology. The blue collar AI strategy the bank has adopted ensures that AI initiatives provide value to the business and that the great majority of them are deployed into production. The bank's AI strategy is clearly focused on improving existing operations and facilitating closer relationships with customers. The clarity of the bank's objectives, of course, makes these objectives much more likely to be achieved.

Influencing Customer Behaviors with Data and AI in Insurance

We've maintained that the least common objective for AI in companies is to change customer behavior. As we've discussed, this objective is quite well along in social media organizations, but is not as advanced in other domains. And as is well known now, social media can change behavior in both positive ways (e.g., creating a feeling of community) and negative ways (e.g., creating social divisiveness).

But in the insurance industry, the goal is to create only positive behavior change. The industry increasingly wants not only to pay its customers when something bad happens in their lives, but also to help them prevent bad things from happening in the first place. These companies are seeking to make a profit, of course, but they want to do so by helping their customers stay healthy and safe.

We've found at least three companies in different segments of that industry that are attempting to change the behavior of their customers and are using AI to do it. All are at the relatively early stages of pursuing this objective, and they are also looking to use AI for operational improvements. Some of these firms are partnering with start-ups to help build these capabilities, while others have developed the necessary capabilities on their own.

Perhaps the furthest along is Progressive Insurance, a company that has long been a pioneer in the use of data and analytics to make customer-oriented decisions. It was the first in the industry to price insurance based on credit scores, and later it was the first to price based on drivers' behaviors. Anthem, which we described in chapter 4, is a very large US health company; Manulife is the largest insurance company in Canada (with businesses in the United States and Asia) offering life and health insurance, annuities, and other financial services.

Motivating better driving at Progressive

Globally, the automobile insurance business is moving toward the idea that actual driving habits are the best way to determine how much a customer should pay for insurance. Called *usage-based insurance* or UBI, this approach uses sensors to measure how and when someone drives, and prices insurance lower for safer drivers and higher for those exhibiting riskier driving behaviors. Progressive introduced this innovation in 2008 with a program that is now called Snapshot.

By now Progressive has captured data on over fourteen billion miles of driving by its Snapshot customers. It uses machine learning models to translate driving behaviors into the prices it charges individual customers. The company has recently adopted automated machine learning (AutoML) so that data scientists can analyze more data and price more efficiently and effectively.

Snapshot monitors different factors in different US states, but among the driving data that Progressive collects (either through a mobile phone or through a device that plugs into the car and transmits data wirelessly) are:

- *Excessive acceleration or deceleration.* Through an accelerometer, Snapshot monitors fast acceleration, strong braking, or hard cornering.

- *Time of day of driving.* Snapshot monitors when customers drive, charging more for insurance when drivers are on the road between midnight and 6:00 am or at rush hours.

- *Distance driven.* Snapshot charges lower prices to drivers who put fewer miles on their vehicles (though it requires at least four thousand miles driven per year).

- *Using a mobile phone.* If the Snapshot app is on the driver's mobile phone, Snapshot can determine whether the driver makes calls or texts while driving, and if so, charges more.

- *Speeding.* Driving above or below speed limits (the mobile device version has a GPS) is recorded by Snapshot and yields lower prices for legal speeds.

Snapshot influences behavior not only through pricing discounts (up to 30 percent), but also through driving safety letter grades (A grades receive large discounts, B smaller discounts, C and below no discount); beeps from the plug-in device when unsafe behaviors are registered;

website reports on driving during trips; and machine learning-generated driving tips on smartphones. Progressive claims that in total, drivers have saved about a billion dollars on their insurance using Snapshot. At some point, it would also be good if the company could compute the likely number of accidents it has helped to prevent.

New health behaviors at Anthem

Anthem announced in 2020 that it planned to become a digital platform for health, to connect the millions of members of its health plans to services to improve their whole health. Rajeev Ronanki, the company's president of digital platforms told us that the goal was to move from "sick care" to "health care": "Rather than treat people who are sick, we will try to keep them healthy." He said the company is trying to connect individual members, employers, and health-care providers in order to create personalized health care and drive healthy behaviors, transforming the focus of care from reactive to proactive and preventive.

Ronanki was quoted in the company's 2020 annual report:

> Seven of the 10 most valuable companies in the world today are platform businesses that have effectively digitized supply and demand. At Anthem, we have built the industry's largest platform, integrating our immense data assets, proprietary AI, and machine-learning algorithms. It's through this platform that we are able to digitize knowledge and create a more agile and seamless experience for our consumers, customers, provider partners, and communities.

The report continues:

> Our platform approach is already having an impact: We've virtualized delivery of care, without needing to acquire expensive brick-and-mortar care delivery infrastructure.

We are able to predict demand for care and connect people to the right care, at the right time—seamlessly blending digital, virtual, and physical care. And we are able to continually optimize supply and demand using our AI and machine-learning capabilities to identify individual health needs that will drive overall health improvement impact at the community level.[1]

As of 2021, Anthem had developed an award-winning app for its members, outfitted with a suite of AI-enhanced tools and services developed to ease care navigation and tailor the care experience to each individual. One of these tools includes the capability to match members to compatible providers, utilizing provided health information, demographic data, and preferences. Anthem also uses its AI capabilities to identify members in need of complex procedures and then guide them to lower-cost, high-quality facilities and services to ease access to care and reduce costs to the member.

Anthem wants to empower members and their communities, placing the control of their health back into their hands. The company understands that health goes beyond the clinical sphere and into the environment that surrounds each person, where everyday behaviors and decisions hold the key to members living better and longer. With most of one's health determined by the community that members live in, Anthem is taking the extra step to partner with companies such as Sharecare to impact whole health. Together, Anthem and Sharecare have developed AI to perform geographic analyses on data from the digital health company's Community Well-Being Index to determine the well-being of communities across the nation and identify opportunities for improvement. At the individual level, Sharecare's AI tailors and suggests lifestyle and habit changes through certified programs and enables personalized outreach and interventions for flagged unfavorable trends. Of course, the goal here is to have the learnings of one benefit the many, transforming community health through integrated and shared information, powered by AI. To achieve this health transformation, health-care researchers can also collect and train their own health data to generate AI models that can positively impact their community in real time.

Anthem understands that while member experience and community engagement are critical in health care, a deeper impact requires the empowerment of the entire health ecosystem. For providers, many of Anthem's AI capabilities live on its provider platform and care management system. Integrated into the clinician workflow, AI-powered insights are available to providers, creating a holistic, 360-degree view of their patients. This view utilizes their health record and other health data sources like health sensors and remote patient monitors. Anthem's AI tools assist clinicians in summarizing and prioritizing patient health interventions across a vast wealth of data, resulting in timely interventions and better health outcomes through more proactive and personalized delivery of care.

In addition to empowering members and providers, the company has developed ways for health plans to identify gaps in care, particularly ones that impact Medicare and Medicaid members. These AI and analytics tools seek to improve risk and quality by performing root-cause analysis for Medicare Advantage and Part D prescription drug plan quality ratings, enabling next best action clinical intervention design, and personalizing outreach to members, ensuring that insights turn into actions.

Anthem is creating holistic artificial intelligence solutions that impact each member's individual health journey and the end-to-end health care experience. Through AI, they are working to personalize care options, simplify care management, and deliver the right care at the right time, and in the right setting. By mid-2021, over a million Anthem members were already using the company's digital concierge, a centralized suite of tools to connect a member with chronic or complex conditions (such as cancer) to their entire care team. Anthem also offers the Total Health, Total You program to employer group members. It helps members create and implement a personalized health improvement plan, including concierge customer service. Supported by AI, customer service interactions are based on predictive modeling that furnishes relevant information to consumers through active voice or chat communications. The behavior change goal is to motivate members to improve their own health.

Anthem has integrated—with its partner Hydrogen Health—a symptom checker for members to input symptoms they are experiencing into the app. The app informs users how other people who experienced similar symptoms were diagnosed. It then provides options for how to learn more, including texting or a telephone call with a doctor or self-treatment. It's already being used by thousands of members, and Anthem expects five million users by 2025.

In chapter 3 we discussed Anthem's partnership with Lark to monitor and attempt to improve its members' health through AI. It is one of many attempts to use data, AI, and relatively automated interventions to teach consumers what healthy behaviors are and try to inculcate them at scale.

Anthem has all the capabilities necessary to excel at AI; it's been focusing on the technology heavily for several years. It has the people, leadership, investments, and other resources to drive both operational improvements and new programs to influence member behaviors. Of course, bringing about change in the behaviors of 43 million members is an ambitious target, and Anthem will be addressing it with AI and other initiatives for some time.

Behavioral insurance at Manulife

Manulife, the Canadian insurance giant with major businesses in the United States and Asia, is taking seriously the idea that insurers should do more than pay customers when they die, have a health problem, or have an accident in their homes or cars. Their goal is to help their customers lead safer, healthier, and better lives. The company has embraced the idea of behavioral insurance, which uses the principles of behavioral economics to change customers' behaviors in positive ways. As we discussed in chapter 3, this is an attempt to use AI and other approaches to change customer behaviors in positive ways.

Manulife is among a few global partners (Ping An is another) with Vitality, a UK-based insurance company that specializes in motivating behavior changes to improve health. The unhealthy behaviors Vitality addresses include insufficient exercise, unhealthy eating habits, smoking, and drinking alcohol to excess. These behaviors increase four noncommunicable diseases (respiratory disease, cancer, diabetes, and cardiovascular disease) that cause 60 percent of early worldwide deaths according to the World Health Organization.

Through the Vitality partnership, Manulife offers members the ability to upload their activity tracker and other data to the company and get rewards (including smartwatch discounts, lower insurance premiums, and discounted travel) for keeping fit. Members can also get discounts on healthy foods at participating retailers. AI is used to deliver personalized nudges to members that are intended to motivate or reward specific behaviors. The most active members among customers using Vitality around the world have mortality rates that are 60 percent lower than average, and serious disease morbidity reductions by 20 to 30 percent.

While there is evidence that these personalized behavioral interventions are working, it's fair to say that we're all in the early days of influencing behavior with AI. We don't yet know how best to motivate and change individual behaviors, what combination of rewards is most effective, and how lasting any behavior changes will be. But it's an admirable effort, and certainly there is too much data, too many predictions to make and prescriptions to fill, to accomplish it successfully without AI. And as we've noted, social media has changed behaviors (for better or worse), and it's also been successful in credit scoring—so why not in insurance?

It's also important to point out that while different archetypes require different capabilities, each of the companies we've described in this chapter uses AI for multiple purposes. Ping An uses AI not only to create new ecosystems and business models, but also to identify and manage risks, and to create operational efficiencies. It's also experimenting with influencing customer behavior. Progressive uses AI not only for its Snapshot usage-based insurance offering, but also for its customer service chatbot based on its popular TV ads. And virtually all these organizations are pursuing automation of back-office tasks.

It's also critical to remember that while these legacy companies are breaking new ground in their industries, they all have startups as competitors. For example, in insurance, startups like Oscar and Lemonade in the United States compete with Anthem and Progressive. In China, Ping An has startup competitors in each of its ecosystems. The fact that the companies we've described in this chapter are building strong AI capabilities doesn't guarantee their long-term survival. But it certainly makes it more likely.

Developing Ethical AI Capabilities

A key aspect of developing AI capabilities is ensuring that AI systems are trustworthy and ethical. This is widely agreed on in principle to be an important area, but actually making it happen is much more challenging. Only a few organizations have the needed structures and processes in place, and most of them are tech organizations. And even these tech companies encounter AI ethics challenges.

Policies and roles at AI vendors

The first step in a responsible AI program is to create policies and responsible roles to oversee the ethical dimension of AI. Most of the companies that have taken this step thus far are vendors of AI products and services—tech or services vendors. Google, Facebook, Micro-soft, Salesforce, IBM, Sony, and DataRobot are all in this category. Most of the officers in charge of AI ethics focus primarily on internal evangelism (related to their products and services) or external preach-ing (to customers) about the importance of AI ethics.[2] Some have developed specific methods to improve or track ethical issues, such as the model cards idea for documenting data sources and algorithmic intent developed at Google and applied at Salesforce and elsewhere.[3] Facebook developed a tool called Fairness Flow to evaluate potential algorithmic bias in machine learning models it has developed.[4]

However, the status of these AI ethics groups at some vendors—particularly at Google—has been somewhat uncertain and unstable. Google fired two AI ethics researchers after they were critical of some of the company's technology, and the remaining employees in that group are reported to be unsure of its direction.[5] Facebook's AI eth-ics have also been publicly questioned. One of its data scientists became a whistleblower although the company maintains a respon-sible AI group.

Despite the controversy and tumult, some organizations have restricted development and marketing of some AI capabilities, at least in part because internal ethics groups or review boards vetoed them. A Reuters report describes several examples: since early last year, Google has also blocked new AI features analyzing emotions, fearing cultural insensitivity, while Microsoft restricted software mimicking voices and IBM rejected a client request for an advanced facial-recognition system.[6]

These examples suggest that the ethics review process at these vendors is working at least to some degree.

Policy content

Many of these organizations, and somewhat fewer nontech organ-izations, have developed ethical or responsible AI policy statements. There is a high degree of consensus in the topics and directions of these policies. Deloitte's Trustworthy AI Framework, which was developed to aid clients in developing their own policies, is a good example of such a policy framework. It has six key elements:

- *Fair and impartial.* Assess whether AI systems include internal and external checks to help enable equitable application across all participants.

- *Transparent and explainable.* Help participants understand how their data can be used and how AI systems make decisions. Algorithms, attributes, and correlations are open to inspection.

- *Responsible and accountable.* Put an organizational structure and policies in place that can help clearly determine who is responsible for the output of AI-system decisions.

- *Safe and secure.* Protect AI systems from potential risks (including cyber risks) that may cause physical and digital harm.

- *Respectful of privacy.* Respect data privacy and avoid using AI to leverage customer data beyond its intended and stated use. Allow customers to opt in and out of sharing their data.

- *Robust and reliable.* Confirm that AI systems have the ability to learn from humans and other systems and produce consistent and reliable outputs.

The framework also has a central core of regulatory compliance and AI governance (figure 5-1).

However, a relatively small number of nonvendor companies—even some AI-first ones—have developed AI ethics roles, policy frameworks, and compliance processes thus far. One is Ping An, which has created an AI ethics governance policy. Ping An's policy emphasizes both human autonomy and human centricity relative to AI, and the company has established an AI ethics committee, a supervisory

FIGURE 5-1

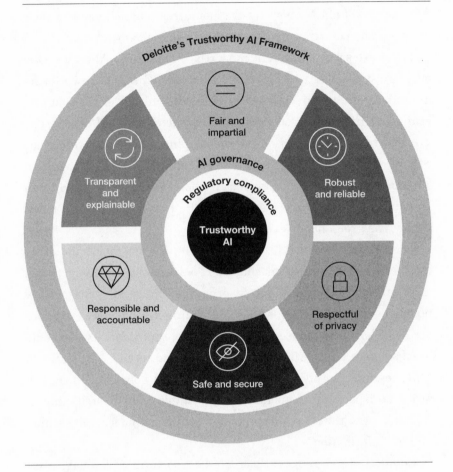

committee, and a project management approach to assess AI applications for their compliance with policy.[7]

Corporate consortia and AI ethics

Some companies choose not (or not only) to go it alone on AI ethics, but
rather to join a consortium of companies oriented to researching and
developing policies on AI ethics. Since many of the topics for AI ethics
are similar across organizations, a consortium can help companies
jump-start their ethics program by creating templates for policies and

briefing papers or conferences in which the key issues are addressed. Although most of the consortia are membership-based, many of their research and policy documents are available to nonmembers.

There are several different consortia that address AI ethics. One of the first to do so was the World Economic Forum (known for its annual conferences in Davos, Switzerland), which over the past several years has addressed many different aspects of AI ethics. The projects include Generation AI: Developing Artificial Intelligence Standards for Children; Responsible Limits on Facial Recognition Technology; and Human-Centred Artificial Intelligence for Human Resources. The WEF has also shared AI ethics principles that members of the group have developed.

The Partnership on AI, formed in 2016, consists of AI and other tech vendors (including Amazon, Google, Facebook, IBM, and Sony), academic institutions, nonprofit organizations, and relatively few nontech companies. Its mission is "bringing diverse voices together across global sectors, disciplines, and demographics so developments in AI advance positive outcomes for people and society."[8] Its staff and affiliates have authored several research and policy documents on different aspects of AI, including algorithmic bias, diversity among AI developers, the role of documentation in machine learning ethics, and misinformation.

EqualAI is a more recently created consortium with a particular focus on "reducing unconscious bias in the development and use of artificial intelligence." Among the tools it has developed are a checklist for identifying bias in AI.[9] It also has the goal of identifying regulatory and legislative solutions.

The Data and Trust Alliance, established in 2020, has a large proportion of nontech employers among its members. Deloitte is a founding member of the consortium of CEOs focused on responsible data practices. One of its goals is to "develop new practices and tools to advance the responsible use of data, algorithms, and AI." The first project that it has identified and begun to address is Algorithmic Safety: Mitigating Bias in Workforce Decisions.

While we believe that working with such consortia can speed the process of identifying ethical AI policies and management frameworks, the customization of them for specific organizations, and most of all their implementation and their ongoing governance in organizations, requires dedicated resources. We expect that many more nontech organizations will need to develop AI ethics approaches as the technology becomes more critical to their businesses. Of course, if a company is featured in this book, AI is already critical to its business—so it should have policies, governance, and leadership roles for AI ethics already in place.

Automation and responsible AI

We've discussed the rise of automated machine learning model creation and MLOps to automatically assess whether machine learning models are no longer predicting well ("drifting") and need to be retrained. But now several vendors of these tools can also examine models automatically to produce model insights that check different aspects of their trustworthiness. An early adopter of these approaches was Chatterbox Labs, a UK-based company that offers automated insights capabilities including the explainability, fairness, privacy, and security vulnerabilities of models and the data they employ. Deloitte's AI Institute uses Chatterbox Labs tools with clients. Other AutoML and MLOps vendors, such as DataRobot and H2O, also have some model bias and fairness evaluation capabilities, and there is also an open-source toolbox called FairML to generate similar model insights.

Implementing ethics policies at Unilever

Of course, it's easier to draft ethical policy statements than to implement them. Most of the companies that have created such policies are also having to carefully consider how best to govern and enforce them. One such company is Unilever, which implemented a set of AI assurance policies in 2022. Drafting the policies was relatively straightforward, and the resulting statements referred to the usual issues of transparency, algorithmic bias, fairness, and so forth. Efficacy is another factor to be desired, which is why the focus is assurance rather than only ethical or responsible AI. As Giles Pavey, Unilever's global data science director who led the assurance effort, put it, "To deliver our business goals we have to do more with less. AI is the foremost tool in this journey but it has to be responsible AI. We need AI assurance so that we can push the barriers of possibilities within the guardrails of responsibility."

The ongoing implementation process for AI assurance was more complex—in part because Unilever is a highly globalized company with somewhat autonomous country-based business units, and because it has many external suppliers of IT applications. Applications that use AI within Unilever could be internally built, built to order by an IT vendor, or embedded within services that Unilever procures from partners. The company's advertising agencies, for example, often employ programmatic buying software that uses AI to decide what digital ads to place on web and mobile sites.

The basic idea behind the Unilever AI assurance compliance process is to examine each new AI application to determine how intrinsically risky the use case is. An application to forecast cash flow, for example, is unlikely to involve any fairness or bias risk, but may have efficacy issues and risk related to explainability. Unilever already has a well-defined approach to information security, and the goal is to employ a similar approach to ensure that no AI application is put into production without first being approved.

When a new AI solution is being planned, the Unilever employee or supplier proposes the outlined use case and method before developing it. This is then reviewed internally, with more complex cases being assessed by external experts. The project proposer is thus informed of potential ethical and efficacy risks and mitigations to be considered. After the AI application has been developed, Unilever (or the external party) runs statistical tests to ascertain whether there is a bias or fairness issue. It can then examine the system for efficacy in achieving its objectives. Depending on where within the company the system will be employed, there also may be local regulations with which the system will have to comply. If the system is judged to be risky, a recommended mitigation approach is communicated. If, for example, a résumé checker used by human resources was fully automated, the review might conclude that the system needs a human in the loop to make final decisions about whether to move to interview. If there are serious risks that can't be mitigated, the AI assurance process rejects the application on the grounds that Unilever's values prohibit using this AI application. Final decisions on AI use cases are made by a senior executive board including representatives from the legal, human resources, and AI departments within Unilever.

A real example of how the process has worked can be seen in the case of a cosmetic brand that Unilever sells through concessions in department stores. The concessionaire required that sales agents in the stores have a certain standard of personal appearance (e.g., the application of makeup on their own faces or length of any facial hair while at work). Unilever wanted a system where agents could prove their attendance at work by sending in a selfie each day to be automatically registered. A stretch objective for this project proposed that the computer vision AI within the system could also detect whether the agent's appearance met with the required standard. In this case the AI assurance process helped the project team think more broadly than the required regulations, legality, and efficacy of such an approach, to also consider the potential implications of such a fully automated system. For instance, should such a system— even if it were proven to be highly accurate—be allowed to automatically demerit a sales agent for noncompliance? After going through this process, it became obvious to the company that they needed to make sure there was a human involved to check the photos that were flagged as noncompliant and deal with any situation that might arise as a result.

Another example where Unilever is studying the responsible use of AI is the use of facial recognition to gain access to its factories. Issues they must consider include making sure the system is robust for all employees regardless of how they look, and that the database of facial coordinates is securely stored. Additionally, it's important to ensure that there is a failsafe system that allows employees to gain access should the AI not recognize a valid worker.

It's clear from these examples that there will be many difficult issues to address for any organization with an AI ethics policy or orientation. Part of AI's power is the ability to deal with customers and employees in a granular fashion that allows different categories of people to be treated differently. But differential treatment can easily shade into bias or unfairness. Both the legal and regulatory environments around ethical and responsible AI, and company policies in advance of or in response to them, are likely to change frequently and dramatically over the next several years. Companies like Unilever that embrace AI will also have to embrace the evolution in the understanding and application of responsible uses of the technology.

CHAPTER 6

Industry Use Cases

We've described the AI strategic archetypes of leading AI adopters and some of the capabilities they have built to realize those objectives. In this chapter we will be much more granular in describing what AI leaders do. We'll focus by industry segment and delve into the specific use cases that AI-fueled companies adopt in order to lead those industries. Use cases—also known as AI applications—are the fundamental unit for describing what a company does with AI. Much of the use case information in this chapter is adapted from the AI Dossier, a document that Deloitte AI experts put together to describe AI leadership from the bottom up—use case by use case, industry by industry.[1]

Choosing and prioritizing use cases is at the heart of any company's AI strategy. AI-powered organizations choose use cases that will differentiate them from competitors (at least for a while), advance their business strategies and models, and fit with their business process designs. Consider this chapter a shopping catalog for AI applications. Not all use cases are covered for every industry—and some use cases can be applied across industries—but it's the most comprehensive list we've seen.

Some of the use cases we'll describe are already becoming table stakes for their industries, and some have been in evidence for a while in less precise and data-driven forms. For each industry we'll also describe some that are emerging or only suited to relatively narrow situations. Our overall goal is to describe what it takes to truly excel with AI, and detail some of the AI use cases that have been adopted by AI-focused organizations in each industry sector.

Consumer Industries

Consumer industries include consumer goods manufacturing, retail, automotive, lodging, restaurants, travel, and transportation. They all serve consumers (though some, like manufacturers, have intermediaries like retailers) and need to understand their preferences and feelings in detail. They all have complex logistical, product/service development, and customer contact challenges that AI can help to address.

Some of the commonly adopted use cases in this segment (with our comments on their application to AI-enabled businesses) include:

- *Fleet network optimization.* AI (as well as other forms of analytics, like operations research) can be used to optimize routes, eliminate or reduce empty backhauling, and maximize flow through distribution centers. Of course, AI has difficulty optimizing supply chains during periods of disruption like the Covid-19 pandemic, but it can provide early warning of supply chain problems for vigilant companies.

- *Next level of personalization.* AI is necessary for highly granular personalization—not just "people who bought this also bought this" collaborative filtering, but machine learning-based predictions of who will buy something or who will respond to an ad or offer based on past customer behaviors. Personalization increasingly also takes a consumer's location, social media posts, and fitness/health behaviors into account—with their permission, of course.

- *Assortment optimization.* AI, and machine learning in particular, are at the heart of modern assortment optimization. These types of models ensure that the right products are available on the shelf with no stockouts. This was particularly difficult during the Covid-19 pandemic, of course. But the most sophisticated AI users found ways to make it happen.

- *Supply and demand planning.* AI-focused retailers, for example, plan for supply and demand almost continuously. The Kroger Co., as we've discussed, does a demand plan for every SKU for every store every night. Assuming normal patterns of demand and supply, machine learning is an excellent tool for planning.

- *Automated customer contact.* Leading firms use chatbots or intelligent agents to manage customer interactions as well. DBS Bank, for example, relentlessly improves its chatbot so that customers have no need or desire to call the customer center. In retail, for example, there are at least twelve different specific use cases, from product search to collecting customer feedback.[2]

Emergent or narrow AI use cases in the consumer segment include the following:

- *Autonomous stores.* Amazon is well known for its cashierless Amazon Go stores (now also in Whole Foods), although stocking and cleaning is still done by humans.[3] Semi-autonomous cashierless stores are also present in Korea—emart24 and Hyundai Uncommon Store are two examples.

- *Autonomous driving.* Fully autonomous vehicles are taking longer to arrive than anticipated, as we discussed in chapter 3. But some "geofenced" areas feature full self-driving, and automated safety devices are proliferating even on relatively inexpensive cars.

- *Fashion tech.* Fashion retailers are increasingly offering AI-based virtual dressing rooms, as well as AI recommendations for styles that the customer might like. Stitch Fix, once an online styling startup that is now a large company, combines AI-based recommendations with a personal stylist.

- *Personalized health, fitness, and wellness.* We described these behavioral health recommendations in chapter 5 relative to insurance companies, but they are driven by consumer devices like smart watches and phones. They can offer personalized nudges to change health behaviors for the better.

- *Service experience modernization.* Shopping and consumer services are increasingly being transformed by AI-driven personalized products and services, recommendations, offers, websites, and mobile apps.

AI in the Walmart supply chain

We haven't discussed Walmart yet in this book, but they may be viewed as one of the most capable consumer businesses and retailers in the use of AI that was born nondigital. The company's supply chain for replenishing physical stores is well known, and it is making considerable progress in e-commerce sales and delivery. Walmart has hundreds of data scientists doing work in supply chain and forecasting/demand management, and it collaborates closely with suppliers on these disciplines. It has a very sophisticated set of "traveling salesman" algorithms for route optimization of its fleet of trucks and delivery vehicles, and uses "tabu search" models run on graphics processing units (GPUs) to optimize supply chain processes. Walmart also uses an AI model to determine the next-best-available option when a customer orders online and a selected product isn't available.

Walmart may have had a relatively late start in automating its warehouses—many built in the 1960s and 1970s—but it is rapidly adding capabilities in that area. It has announced it is spending $14 billion to redesign its distribution centers and employ new technologies, including AI and robotics. The company is working with Symbotic, a robot manufacturer created by former executives at Amazon Robotics, to improve its warehouse automation. It also uses robots to load different sizes of boxes in cubes (that the robots figure out how to create) for delivery to stores. Walmart is even partnering with Ford's Argo AI unit to pilot self-driving delivery vehicles for online orders in three US cities. It has also experimented with robots in stores to identify stockouts or mis-shelved items, and with other robots to clean floors.

Walmart's distribution and delivery services are now not just an internal capability. It created the GoLocal service for other retailers that want to offer same- or next-day delivery. One of its first partners for the service was Home Depot. Like UPS and FedEx, it is becoming a significant provider of shipping services in addition to its retailing prowess.

Energy, Resources, and Industrials Industries

The energy, resources, and industrials industry segment includes many large companies with substantial capital budgets, but for a variety of reasons many have not heavily embraced AI—yet. These organizations are largely business-to-business providers, and they sometimes don't have enough customer data to employ a lot of machine learning models. Many industrial organizations use AI applications, but these can be difficult to integrate with machinery or factories on a large scale. However, despite these obstacles, leading companies are making considerable progress with some AI use cases.

Relatively common use cases for this segment include:

- *Predictive asset maintenance.* This was one of the first AI use cases in industrial companies, and is still the most popular. It predicts a need for maintenance based on sensors that indicate the early signs of a failure, or conditions that could lead to one. AI-powered companies like Shell do this on a grand scale—they already have ten thousand pieces of machinery monitored for signs of trouble, and are heading toward many more.

- *Edge AI for production and planning.* Companies are increasingly placing sensors at the edges of their networks and using AI to analyze the data that comes from them. Sensors can detect or measure flow, temperature, chemicals in the atmosphere, sound, or images. Shell is using autonomous drones to monitor pipeline condition through image recognition—a form of both edge AI and predictive maintenance. It is also using machine learning-based computational fluid dynamics to plan wind farms and optimize production of them when built. The Danish energy company Ørsted also makes extensive use of data and AI to optimize production of energy from its over fifteen hundred wind turbines.[4]

- *Field sensor data analysis.* The primary industry that makes use of field sensors is the energy industry, which uses them extensively in oil and gas exploration. Sensors in drill bits, for example, monitor heat and vibration, and can predict imminent breakage. Mobile phone images of drill bits can be examined with deep learning models to assess wear and underground soil composition. In windmills, sensors can provide data for AI systems to optimize blade angles and rotation speed.

- *Field workforce and safety.* AI can be used to make hazardous work safer. For example, at Southern California Edison, a predictive model scores the likelihood of a safety risk for each field maintenance or installation project, and the field teams discuss how to lower the risk for high-scoring projects. The model is integrated with the company's work order system.

- *Utility service outage prediction.* Electrical utilities can use machine learning models to generate outage risk scores for grid assets and circuits in a service territory with the goal of reducing customer interruption minutes. The risks assessed can include fire, weather, animal interference, and vegetation. Southern California Edison's primary focus for such prediction is wildfires, and it uses image recognition analysis from drone footage as well as broader machine learning models to predict the risk of fires and shut down circuits in advance of them.

Some emerging or narrow use cases for AI in this segment include:

- *Materials informatics.* University and industrial researchers are beginning to use AI to understand how new combinations of chemicals and compounds can create high-performance materials.

- *Algorithmic supply chain planning.* Supply chain optimization is generally based on continuation of existing trends in demand and supply, but AI is beginning to be used to predict potential disruptions to supply chains, including pandemics, political unrest, and shipping bottlenecks.

- *Digital twin factory.* Digital twins are virtual replicas of machinery and even entire factories that are continually updated with data. AI detects anomalies and addresses malfunctions in machines. This is a more comprehensive and detailed approach to predictive asset maintenance.

- *Virtual plant operator assistant.* Plant floor workers and supervisors typically roam floors to intervene with machines, but many of their tasks will soon be replaced by AI systems that make automated adjustments. Augmented reality devices (which themselves use AI) will work in concert with machine learning applications. Airbus is using AI software to do this already in its Harbin Hafai Airbus joint venture in China.

AI-enabled quality at Seagate

One high-tech manufacturer is Seagate Technologies, the world's largest disk drive manufacturer. It has massive amounts of sensor data in its factories and has been using it extensively over the last five years to ensure and improve the quality and efficiency of its manufacturing processes.

One of the primary foci for Seagate's manufacturing analytics has been the automation of visual inspection of silicon wafers, from which disk drive heads are made, and of the tools to manufacture them. Multiple microscope images are taken from various toolsets throughout wafer fabrication, and these images play a key role in detecting faults within the wafer and monitoring the health of the toolsets. Seagate's Minnesota factory utilized the data provided by these images to create an automated fault detection and classification system with the ability to detect and classify wafer defects directly from the image. Other image classification models detect out-of-focus electron microscopes in tools, ensuring that any defects are actual and not out-of-focus images.[5]

Based on deep learning image recognition algorithms, these auto defect classification models were first deployed in late 2017, and since then the scale and power of image analysis has grown extensively across the company's wafer factories in the United States and Northern Ireland, realizing multimillion-dollar savings in inspection labor and scrap prevention. While the company has been able to reduce the number of manual inspections using these systems, the goal has been not just to free up inspection labor for other types of work, but also to make manufacturing processes more efficient. Visual inspection accuracy was at 50 percent several years ago but now exceeds 90 percent.

Seagate also worked with Google Cloud, a major customer that employs millions of disk drives, to predict hard drive failures before they fail in large data centers. The resulting model was successful, and engineers now have a larger window to identify failing disks. That not only allows them to reduce costs, but also enables prevention of problems before they impact end users.[6]

Financial Services Industries

Financial services—including banking, insurance, investment management, and trading—have been the industries that are most active in the use of AI. It's an information-rich sector, rapid and accurate decisions are critical to its success, and its customers need substantial amounts of advice to live more successful financial lives. Financial services organizations also typically have the financial resources to invest in AI. It's not surprising, then, that more of the AI-first organizations we describe in this book are in financial services than any other industry sector.

Some of the specific use cases that are already popular in financial services include:

- *Legal and compliance analytics.* Banks need to control fraud for their own financial purposes, but also are required to engage in "know your customer" and anti–money laundering activities for regulatory purposes. AI—in the form of decision rule systems—has been used in the industry for many years for fraud reduction, but those capabilities, which tended to create too many false positive alerts, are now supplemented by machine learning capabilities. DBS Bank, for example, added machine learning to its transaction surveillance capabilities, which allows it to rank suspicious transactions in terms of their likelihood of needing investigation. The new system improved both analysts' productivity by a third in reviewing positive cases, as well as letting them use more data. The least likely cases are put into hibernation and not reviewed at all unless the customer has additional suspicious activity.

- *Conversational AI.* AI-enabled chatbots or intelligent agents, of course, are increasingly common in banking. They aren't particularly exciting if all they do is allow a customer to check a balance. But banks are increasingly adding other, more sophisticated capabilities to their conversational AI systems. Erica, Bank of America's chatbot, has grown steadily in usage to over twenty million customers in under three years of operation. In addition to basic capabilities like balance checking, it points out spending anomalies, gives advice about saving for goals that the customer has established, and can process more than sixty thousand phrases and questions related to Covid-19. The chatbot has also been made chattier and more personable over time.

- *360° customer experience.* Banks are using AI and other digital tools to better understand and improve the customer experience. By now, many have used customer journey analysis to learn what the customer experience is truly like for customers, and machine learning models predict when a difficult customer experience is likely to antagonize a customer or lead to attrition. Unsupervised learning models can identify new or poorly served segments using cluster analysis. Next-best-action systems like the one we've described at Morgan Stanley use machine learning to identify the financial products or services that are most likely to be valued by customers. The bank or insurance company that lacks customer knowledge no longer has the excuse of inadequate technology.

- *Insurance underwriting.* Insurance underwriting has long been based on rule engines, but leading companies are combining or replacing rules with machine learning applications that can make more data-based and precise underwriting decisions. This trend is taking place in commercial and home property insurance, using AI-based image recognition of roof condition or nearby trees. It's being used in automobile insurance, allowing drivers to take photos of their vehicles before they are insured (and after an accident, for no-touch claims adjudication and payment—as we'll describe in the next chapter). It's happening in life insurance as well, as these companies attempt to avoid expensive and inconvenient medical exams before they underwrite policies. Haven Life, for example, a unit of MassMutual insurance, has a digital underwriting approach that enables half of all applications to require no human review; 20 percent of accepted applications need no medical exam.[7]

- *Usage-based insurance.* As we discussed in chapter 5, charging differential insurance rates based on how customers drive was pioneered by Progressive Insurance in 2008. Now many companies, both startups and established organizations, use the technology, which requires AI to analyze all the data and determine recommendations for improved driving behaviors as well as underwriting implications.

- *Trade operations automation.* Many financial trades are already processed and cleared through straight-through processing with no human touch, but there are many failed trades requiring substantial human intervention. AI is both making those less likely and helping to resolve the trades needing further investigation. It can predict trades that are likely to fail and require more data before they do so, extract information from trade documents that can resolve failed or problematic trades, and detect patterns and anomalies in trade data that can be very useful to traders.

- *Consumer fraud detection.* Detecting fraud in banking and insurance is a major use case area, with AI playing a central role. Credit card companies, for example, attempt to identify fraud before the transaction is approved at the point of sale. Scoring a transaction for fraud requires both machine learning and close integration with transactional systems.

- *Credit risk analytics.* Using AI to determine whether a customer should receive credit is one of the earliest applications of neural networks, beginning with Robert Hecht-Nielsen's innovations in neural network modeling and application in the mid-1980s. Now many different forms of machine learning are used for this purpose.

There are also emergent or narrow use cases that some financial services firms around the world are using:

- *Biometric digital payments.* Using facial recognition to verify customer identity for payments, loans, and insurance policies is already in fairly broad use in China, including at Ping An.

- *Real estate price estimation and prediction.* Most homeowners have checked the Zestimates offered by Zillow, which are machine learning–based predictions of how much the house is worth. Several other real estate sites now have similar capabilities, and insurance companies have versions to value homes before insuring them. However, Zillow's recent closure of its business that bought and sold houses suggests that AI price estimation algorithms may have difficulties in highly variable markets.

AI use cases at Capital One

One of the AI-powered organizations in financial services that we have not yet discussed is Capital One, the third-largest credit card issuer in the United States in terms of balances. That company, with its credo of "information-based strategy" was analytical from its inception as a separate company in 1994. Over the past decade it has also become a powerhouse in machine learning, with use cases that cut across consumer banking functions. We'll describe Capital One's journey from analytics to AI in the next chapter.

The bank has excelled for many years at one key prediction: whether a customer will pay back credit card loans. In addition, however, it uses machine learning to make many other types of predictions:

- Diagnosing mobile phone app failure

- Identifying suspicious transactions for possible money laundering

- Identifying fraudulent credit card transactions and reducing false positive fraud alerts

- Identifying fraudulent digital banking sessions

- Creating virtual card numbers for individual merchants with frequent transactions

- Predicting customer intent in online sessions

- Predicting whether a customer will call the call center, and what problem they will want help with

Capital One also has a capable chatbot, called Eno, that can perform many banking transactions, and inform customers with insights on their spending habits if they want them. The company is also attempting to push the frontier of credit decisioning by using deep learning models and working to make them more explainable and acceptable to regulators. As we'll discuss in the next chapter, Capital One is applying AI in many different areas across the bank.

Government and Public Services Industries

In the United States, government and public service organizations got off to a slow start in adopting AI, at least outside the military and intelligence sectors. There are, however, plenty of use cases in the sector, and some organizations are beginning to adopt them.

Well-established use cases in the sector include:

- *Claims processing back-office automation.* Government organizations often pay claims to individuals or organizations, and AI can help with multiple aspects of it. Robotic process automation is one of the stronger AI capabilities of the US federal government, with a large community of practice across fifty different agencies, and many projects in production. Machine learning can help with paying claims by identifying the most important or easiest-to-pay claims for earlier payment.

- *Population risk support.* This AI-based approach to identifying citizens at risk—of physical and mental health issues, homelessness, or food insecurity—is a way of getting out in front of social problems before they happen. It is furthest along in the health domain. For example, in the UK, medical practitioners are informed when elderly patients score high on a machine learning–based Electronic Frailty Index, and these people receive extra care.

- *Biomedical data science.* The intersection of biology with machine learning is exploding, with researchers attempting to tie diseases and effective treatments to genomics, proteomics, and other disciplines. For example, the Broad Institute, a research organization affiliated with Harvard and MIT, is setting up a $250 million center to connect biology and machine learning. In government, the US National Institutes of Health (NIH) has a number of programs underway to advance the use of AI in basic and applied health research.

- *Benefits administration.* In both the public and private sectors, organizations are increasingly using AI to decide what benefits to provide to citizens and employees. In Denmark, for example, public benefits (including pensions, child allowances, unemployment support, and other social welfare payments) are made in part on the basis of algorithms that determine who receives them. In many private sector companies, human resource organizations are attempting to move toward the "workforce of one" approach, using the same approaches to determine employee benefits that companies use in personalizing offers for customers.

- *Health and environmental predictions.* The success of Blue Dot, a Canadian AI startup, in recognizing the onset and spread of the Covid-19 pandemic has made many epidemiologists aware of the possibilities for predicting disease spread before it gets out of control. AI is also being used by governments to predict volcanic eruptions, floods, avalanches, and other natural disasters.

- *Video surveillance analysis.* Many governments around the world are making use of AI-based video and image recognition for public safety applications. The proliferation of video surveillance cameras has led to a pressing need to automatically analyze their images—not just to solve crimes in the past, but to anticipate and prevent them before they happen.

Some emerging or narrow uses of AI in the government and public service sector include:

- *Agent-based simulations for military strategy.* It's possible that wars of the future will be fought and won on the basis of AI capabilities. In the present, an important application of AI is to simulate battles with intelligent agents. Agent-based simulations often produce more accurate and fruitful war games because they model the behaviors of many agents and can simulate emergent behaviors. Multiple governments are also exploring the use of AI for autonomous control of weaponry. This may include drones and self-driving vehicles, as well as the use of robots as scouts and reconnaissance platforms (airborne or on land).

- *Civil asset and infrastructure management.* Keeping a city or state's infrastructure running effectively is increasingly too complex for humans to do on their own. Public organizations like the Singapore Land Transport Agency are using sensor data and AI to monitor and predict public transportation service outages and recommend the best alternatives for service recovery.[8]

- *Legal outcome predictions.* A valuable but controversial application of AI is in the judicial sphere, in which the decisions of judges and juries can be predicted (typically by lawyers, which may hasten settlements) and augmented by AI. The most well-known use of AI by judges is in algorithmic sentencing recommendations, some versions of which have been associated with bias and lack of transparency.[9]

- *Adaptive learning in education.* Educational institutions, particularly those with substantial online educational content, can employ AI-based adaptive learning tools to monitor how well students are learning and recalling content. Students can be provided with material that is at an appropriate level based on their learning. It's a means of personalizing the learning process, which human instructors can find difficult or impossible to do at scale.

AI in the US Government

The US government, despite a slow start, has come on strong in recent years in both the civilian and defense uses of the technology. A study commissioned by the Administrative Conference of the United States found that as of February 2020, nearly half of federal agencies (45 percent) had experimented with AI and related machine learning tools. Executive Order 13859, Maintaining American Leadership in Artificial Intelligence, followed the study and required federal agencies to create publicly available inventories of use cases of AI. Some of these include:

- NASA launched RPA pilot projects in accounts payable and receivable, IT spending, and human resources. Through the project, 86 percent of these human resources transactions were completed without human intervention.[10]

- The National Oceanic and Atmospheric Administration (NOAA) has deployed an AI strategy to "expand the application of [AI] in every NOAA mission area by improving the efficiency, effectiveness, and coordination of AI development and usage across the agency."[11]

- The Social Security Administration has used AI and machine learning in its adjudication work to address challenges from high caseloads and to ensure accuracy and consistency of decision-making.[12]

- The Department of Veteran's Affairs (VA) established a National Artificial Intelligence Institute to develop AI R&D capabilities in the VA. At the start of the Covid-19 crisis, the VA also implemented AI chatbots to field questions and help determine the severity of confirmed cases and potential locations for patient admission.[13]

- The National Institute for Justice supported research on crime-fighting AI to help investigators sort through data which "could be used to fight human trafficking, illegal border crossings, drug trafficking, and child pornography."[14]

- The Transportation Security Lab (TSL) at the Department of Homeland Security Science and Technology Directorate is actively exploring ways to incorporate AI and machine learning into the TSA security-screening process to improve passenger and bag scanning. TSL is developing new tools, methods, and procedures to test and train algorithms effectively and efficiently before they are commercialized and eventually to reduce rates of false alarms.[15]

- The Internal Revenue Service is using AI to test which combinations of formal notices and contacts are most likely to get a taxpayer who owes money to send a check.[16]

In terms of defense applications, the Department of Defense was estimated to spend $874 million on AI in fiscal 2022 (which began in October 2022).[17] The Pentagon's AI initiatives in that year will number about six hundred—about double the number in fiscal 2021. The Joint AI Center at the DoD was established in 2018 to accelerate the DoD's adoption and integration of AI to achieve mission impact at scale. Through Joint AI Center programs the DoD is leveraging AI applications to support military personnel with health care innovations, transform the character of warfare, improve fleet readiness systems, and support process improvements. The US government, of course, also spends considerable sums on AI for intelligence purposes, though both the level of spending and specific use cases are confidential.

AI in the Singapore Government

Singapore, despite its small size, is often an early adopter of new technology for government and public service, and AI is no exception. The city-state is using AI across a variety of agencies and public service domains, including the Singapore Land Transport Agency we mentioned earlier in this chapter. Other use cases for AI include a system for completing complex tax returns, mobile robots for police and water reservoir surveillance, automated monitoring of temperatures with smartphones to detect Covid-19 infections, self-driving cars and taxis on Singapore streets, and a set of systems for healthcare diagnosis and treatment.

In 2017 the government funded AI Singapore, "a national program in Artificial Intelligence (AI) to catalyze, synergize and boost

Singapore's AI capabilities to power our future, digital economy."[18] This program works with research institutions, companies, and government agencies to accelerate AI development and deployment. It has created and funded research centers in cybersecurity, synthetic biology, marine science, and several other AI-oriented research programs through the National Research Foundation. Based on positive results, the government has funded this program for a second five-year period and has substantially increased other government funding for AI. The government has also founded five research centers of excellence in Singapore universities.

Singapore is also unusual in having established an ethical framework for financial services firms operating in the country. Called the Veritas Consortium, it is led by the Monetary Authority of Singapore and is developing use cases (including open source code) to allow companies to evaluate the fairness of their offerings. It has already completed use cases in credit risk scoring and customer marketing, and plans many more.[19]

Many governments, including the United States and China, have now realized that AI will be critical to future operations. But Singapore was early to the game, and for its size has devoted considerable resources to being a leader in AI and an early adopter of AI use cases in government.

Life Sciences and Health-Care Industries

Life sciences and health-care companies are poised on the edge of a dramatic transformation driven by AI. However, they are not quite there yet. Big pharma companies use AI on the margins but haven't yet fully solved how to develop and test drugs *in silico*, or by computer modeling. There are several promising AI-first startups in drug development, but they haven't made any dramatic breakthroughs yet. In health care, there are daily announcements of advances in the ability of AI to diagnose or predict disease, but few have made it into clinical practice. But use cases in life sciences and health care abound (more than in any other industry sector in our analysis); here are some that are rapidly becoming mainstream:

- *Digital data flow for clinical trials.* Automating clinical trial processes can provide both economic value and faster speed to market for new drug compounds. Most trials are conducted using digital platforms, which allows AI-based analysis and automation of key phases. Pharma companies, often in combination with contract research organizations, are evolving how trials are performed. AI-based synthetic control arms in trials allow individuals not enrolled in trials to serve as controls, which in turn allows more trial participants to receive the experimental therapy. AI can also help to integrate and reconcile trial data, which can speed up trials.

- *Drug manufacturing intelligence.* Pharmaceutical manufacturing processes are becoming more digital and automated, which allows AI to be used to monitor for anomalies and predict process outcomes. AI can identify process degradation and its implications for product quality, monitor discrepancies in material properties, and analyze environmental conditions—all based on sensor data. Digital twins of particular machines and (eventually) entire factories can be created for purposes of predictive asset maintenance and anomaly detection.

- *Drug marketing omnichannel engagement.* Pharmaceutical salesforces are moving past outdated approaches to health-care practitioner marketing, and past television commercials for patient marketing. Savvy digital consumers and practitioners are expecting personalized omnichannel interactions, with AI orchestrating what content is delivered through what channel. These marketing tasks have become much too complex to leave to human marketers alone.

- *"Voice of the patient" insight.* Health-care and life science customers in the past were largely anonymous, but patients now are commenting about their journeys and experiences in social media and in community forums such as Patients Like Me. AI can be used to monitor patient sentiment and discussion topics in online contexts, eventually leading to more positive patient experiences.

- *Proactive risk and compliance. Pharmacovigilance* is becoming increasingly complex, with proof of regulatory compliance required at many stages of a drug development and marketing practice. AI can assist in compliance by identifying problems raised in the general public and practitioner communities and by monitoring news feeds. AI can also be used to assist in post-market surveillance of drugs through side effects and negative outcomes identified in real-world evidence datasets.

- *Patient engagement.* Lack of patient engagement with clinical treatments and nonadherence to medication are major problems for health-care providers and payers. As we discuss in chapters 5 and 7, there are behavioral "nudges" that can be supplied to increase engagement and adherence, particularly when the nudge is personalized to the individual. These next-best-health-care actions require AI just as the consumer offer versions do.

- *Health-care revenue cycle optimization and efficiency.* Both health-care providers and payers are attempting to create more efficient and effective processes for paying for health care, and are increasingly automating care authorizations and payment checks. Machine learning can also be used to accurately estimate patient bills before treatment—now required by law in the United States.

- *Computer-assisted diagnosis.* AI-based diagnosis of some diseases, and automated treatment recommendations, are not new and were present to some degree in rule-based clinical decision support systems. Machine learning, however, is beginning to make diagnosis and treatment much more precise and data based. In particular, deep learning–based image recognition has proven to be as good as or better than human radiologists in detecting medical problems in images. A few of these approaches have been approved by regulatory bodies, but most are still in the lab rather than at the clinical bedside. However, there are many more to come, and we can expect much greater integration of them with clinical processes.

- *Precision medicine and personalized health.* Machine learning is also the key to precision medicine—recommendation of personalized treatments for diseases based on the patient's genetic makeup, key metabolic data, and other factors. Precision medicine is already a reality for cancer patients where the genetic makeup of their tumors and gene-specific treatment strategies are available. Some AI is being used to recommend specific drugs and clinical trials based on genetics. Although this is a long journey, we expect that many more precision medicine approaches will soon become available.

- *Hospital management.* Modern hospitals are expensive collections of facilities, machinery, and talented people, and AI is already playing a role in optimizing their allocation. Emergency rooms, radiological imaging machines, and surgeons are examples of scarce resources that AI has already helped to schedule more efficiently. It seems likely that such optimization will eventually extend to the whole range of health options in health systems, including local clinics, rehabilitation centers, and home care.

There are also a variety of AI use cases that are still primarily in research labs or in very limited clinical use. They include:

- *Biomarker discovery.* Biomarkers are detectable substances that indicate the presence of disease or medical condition. Finding biomarkers is something of a fishing expedition, but in many medical fields, including cancer, there is voluminous data that can yield potential biomarkers. Machine learning allows researchers to find individual and in-combination biomarkers much more quickly and easily. New AI algorithms that predict patterns of protein folding are likely to be used to generate new types of biomarkers.

- *Synthetic biology.* Creating new organisms, devices, or drugs has been a time-consuming process, but AI is likely to speed it up dramatically. New algorithms can predict how changes in a cell's DNA or biochemistry will affect its behavior. These predictive models are likely to speed up not only health care research, but also consumer products like artificial meat.

- *Virtualized drug discovery lab.* Machine learning helps pharmaceutical companies develop digital models of new compounds and predictions of how they will act on specific target molecules. Combined with 3D simulation, it's possible to dramatically speed up drug development time by developing simulated compounds that can eventually be tested and validated on animal and human subjects.

- *Self-healing medical supply chains.* Hospital and medical supplies are subject to the same uncertainties that other products face, although the consequences of late deliveries and stockouts can be much more consequential. Machine learning models can better predict demand and allow rapid re-planning when unanticipated events occur.

- *Digital health-care providers.* Health-care companies are providing a wide variety of intelligent medical assistance services to help and augment the activities of human clinicians. Particularly in China, intelligent telemedicine systems like Ping An's Good Doctor provide suggested support and assistance diagnoses, treatment strategies, and drug recommendations to physicians. Although not well established yet in the United States, such intelligent telemedicine services are likely the future of routine health care.

- *Predictive behavioral models for clinical trials.* A problem for companies conducting clinical trials is that up to 30 percent of trial participants drop out before the trial is concluded. This increases expense, complicates analysis, and may lead to attrition bias. Life sciences organizations are beginning to use machine learning models to predict how likely a trial participant is to complete the trial, and are enrolling only the most likely to do so.

- *Digital pathology.* Thus far pathology has been well behind radiology in adopting AI-based analysis of its images. Many pathologists still prefer microscopes, and pathology has lacked a common data standard for capturing and transmitting images. This situation is beginning to change, and there are several providers of deep learning–based image recognition for pathology cell images. They have not yet been approved by the FDA for analysis without human review, but they are useful for image preclassification and workflow prioritization.

- *Patient vitals monitoring.* Smartwatches that track fitness activities are now common, but they are increasingly also monitoring a variety of medically relevant data, from heart rates to blood oxygen levels to electrocardiogram signals. Some of the data from these devices can be transmitted into electronic health records for long-term monitoring, and these watches can also automatically alert a physician of a serious medical problem.

- *Medication compliance and remote patient monitoring.* Adherence to prescribed medications is a substantial problem for the entire health-care system, but particularly for clinical trials. The "electronic medicine cabinet" is not yet a reality, but some clinical trials are making use of image recognition for smartphone images to show that the patient is taking the drug (or placebo) at the prescribed frequency.

- *Diagnostic image enhancement in radiology.* Deep learning-based image recognition is increasingly successful in research labs, but it has not been widely adopted in clinical practice. One way to increase adoption is to enhance images so that problematic areas are highlighted by the system, or by pointing out features of the image that are not easily visible to the naked eye. Researchers are also working on increasing the reproducibility of image recognition across medical institutions and clinical settings.

AI at the Cleveland Clinic

In our view, AI-fueled legacy organizations in the health-care and life sciences industries don't yet exist. There are plenty of startups that are clearly powered by AI, and a number of both large health-care providers and big pharma companies are active in AI. But we don't think they have reached the point of using AI to significantly transform their businesses. For that reason, we'll describe some of the more aggressive organizations and some of the use cases they have adopted.

In the health-care sector, some of the organizations known for providing innovative, high-quality care are also developing innovative and high-quality AI use cases. Cleveland Clinic, for example, has "AI popping up all over the place," according to Chris Donovan, executive director of enterprise information management and analytics. His group is trying both to facilitate the bottom-up efforts to develop and deploy AI, while also providing governance approaches. The work thus far has been driven by a cross-organizational community of practice anchored in the enterprise analytics, IT, and ethics departments.

The primary benefit of most use cases is operational—making decisions faster and with greater precision. For example, Cleveland Clinic is in the process of implementing a preoperative patient risk score for anesthesia. It has used a rule-based score for many years, but the score is now based on machine learning and is more automated and precise. The hospital also uses enterprise resource-planning system data in finance along with machine learning models to get a better estimate of financial risk. In many administrative functions they are creating more forecasts, predictive models, and simulations with machine learning.

In the population health area, the clinic has built a predictive model that helps prioritize the use of care management resources. Care management resources are scarce, and prioritization of their caseloads is critical to delivering care to the patients most in need. The predictive risk score is now the primary method for determining who gets a check-in call. A diabetic patient that has difficulty in managing the disease, for example, would get a high-risk score. The clinic built another model to identify patients who are at risk for a disease but as yet have no history or symptoms of it. The model is used to try to head off the disease in the patients with high scores by proactively scheduling them for screening or preventive care.

There is yet another predictive model to identify patients with problematic social determinants of health; this is a cohort of patients who may need a social worker as much as a physician, or a bus pass to get to doctor appointments. Donovan said that the model's scores are now done outside of the hospital's electronic health record (EHR) system, but he expects they will eventually be built into the EHR. Any predictive models in the EHR system thus far don't typically perform well, in part because they aren't trained on the clinic's own data.

A substantial number of applications at Cleveland Clinic involve deep learning-based analysis of medical images. Radiologists in the clinic's Imaging Institute are experimenting with the automated identification of cancers and bone fractures, for example, and neurologists are using the technology to help identify the source of epileptic seizures. The current goal of the AI models is to assist the physician in identifying problems in images, and not to perform on a standalone basis. In another medical imaging project, the clinic has also recently announced a partnership with Path AI that seeks to digitize and leverage its pathology slide collection to power AI-driven translational research and clinical diagnostics in multiple disease areas.

Donovan feels that there is tremendous potential to apply AI at Cleveland Clinic, but the biggest challenge involves data. He said that other industries have much more data, and it is more likely to be clean and well structured. Like other hospitals, he said, their data has quality issues, is captured poorly, is entered in different ways, and involves different definitions across the institution. Even a common metric like blood pressure can be taken while the patient is standing, sitting, or supine—typically with different outcomes—and the data is recorded in different ways. Knowledge of the data structures is required to employ the appropriate reading. As a result, data preparation is now a part of each AI project, and Donovan's group is working to provide useful datasets to AI projects as a common service.

Finally, Donovan pointed out that Cleveland Clinic is also taking significant time to understand the ethical considerations related to these technologies. He expects that such deliberations will be key to the wide-scale implementation of them in clinical decision-making.

AI at various big pharma companies

The pharmaceutical or life sciences companies that are attempting to redesign drug development with AI are primarily startups. Time will tell whether they will be successful at improving on that very expensive and time-consuming process. Several big pharma organizations are working diligently on applying AI to their businesses and are employing a wide variety of use cases, but many of their projects are a bit less at the core of drug discovery processes. In other words, they may not be fully AI fueled, but they are attempting to ensure that they can be in the future.

Pfizer, for example, excels at sales and marketing, and many of its AI applications support those functions. Several use cases have involved identifying the types of physicians that are most likely to assist patients with prescribed Pfizer medications, or to inform physicians about the appropriate use of products. Pfizer's Australian business unit is using an AI platform to simulate the impact of alternative sales and marketing strategies. AI also allows the company to personalize communications with patients who are participating in clinical trials. Pfizer is laying the groundwork for more aggressive use of AI in drug discovery and development by creating a scientific data cloud and using it to create algorithms that improve compound prediction. The company used AI methods to accelerate the clinical trials used in the record-setting Covid-19 vaccine it markets with its partner BioNtech. Pfizer is also training employees around the company in AI methods in a series of boot camps.

Novartis is quite public in discussing its AI initiatives. Its AI Innovation Lab, working in partnership with Microsoft, is addressing such use cases as intelligent design of effective and efficient molecules, personalizing viruses that turn the body's T-cells into cancer-fighting agents, and precision dosing for age-related macular degeneration treatments. It is using AI to extract findings from real-world data to suggest opportunities for research and development. The company is also developing a deep learning model to speed up leprosy detection by analyzing images of skin lesions.

AstraZeneca has a collection of both drug discovery and commercial use cases. On the discovery side, its focus is to use large data-sets to predict and rank which molecules might have an impact on disease targets. They're in the process of dramatically speeding up the drug development process with this approach. The next step in the process is to synthesize the molecules in the lab; tools like protein folding prediction are making it possible to speed up this process. Pathologists are using AI to accelerate the process of tissue and cell analysis by up to 30 percent. Automation technologies, both physical robots and process automation, help to accelerate the repeated cycles of generating, analyzing, and testing new compounds. And the company is using federated electronic health record data to speed up clinical trials.

AstraZeneca is also using AI effectively in the commercial side of the business. During the Covid-19 pandemic, for example, it used machine learning and natural language processing to personalize digital communications to physicians—the only way it could communicate at the time. It also has an AI model to evaluate coaching conversations between sales managers and salespeople.

Eli Lilly uses AI for clinical trial development. Lilly's Design Hub Analytics Initiative (DHAI) transforms this process with an innovative technology platform of integrated data sources, advanced analytics, AI, automation, and user experience improvements to analyze alternative trial designs. Machine learning is used to capture and process Lilly's trial experience and other data sources to guide protocol construction and delivery choices such as country and investigator selection. DHAI is already cutting timelines by up to 20 percent, allowing Lilly to bring drug to market substantially faster.

Since dramatic innovations in drug development are often found in smaller startups that are eventually acquired by large pharmaceutical companies, it seems likely that the same pattern will take place with AI. Many big pharma players (including the ones we've described) already have development partnerships with these startups. And if Exscientia, Insilico Medicine, Berg Health, Benevolent AI, and the multiple other AI-focused startups succeed in dramatically improving the speed and effectiveness of drug development, there is little doubt that the practice will make its way into large organizations.

Technology, Media, and Telecommunications Industries

The technology-related industries that Deloitte professionals often refer to as TMT comprise some of the most digital and AI-powered businesses in any sector. Their products and services leave a trail of data—product usage, location, level of interest and attention—that can easily be analyzed with AI. The telecommunications industry, for example, pioneered the use of data mining, and then later the use of machine learning to predict churn, or customer attrition. However, the tech sector is also the industry that often raises the most concern among consumers and policymakers about data privacy, consumer targeting, and surveillance capitalism. How TMT companies deal with these issues over the next several years and balance them with the potential of AI will set the tone for many other industries.

Some common use cases for AI adopters are:

- *Smart factory and digital supply network.* AI is increasingly being applied to manufacturing in the industry that enables AI—semiconductor and computer production. Common use cases include demand forecasting and inventory level predictions, equipment scheduling, chip design automation and design defect identification, yield optimization, and defect identification (as in the Seagate example we discussed earlier in the chapter; it is both a manufacturing company and a technology company).

- *Direct consumer engagement.* Tech industries are among the primary users of tech-oriented marketing and sales. Cisco Systems, for example, developed machine learning–based sales propensity models by the tens of thousands that consider individual customers' likelihood to buy certain products, even though they are B2B companies.[20] Tech organizations also monitor leads carefully, prioritize them with machine learning, and often use natural language processing systems to cultivate low-value or low-likelihood leads.

- *Digital contact center.* Many industries are using chatbots and intelligent agents today, but among the most active are technology-oriented companies. In this industry, natural language processing–based digital agents are used for administrative tasks involving bills and appointments. However, because technology products and services are complex, this industry certainly leads in the use of AI for customer support. Such use cases can not only answer typical customer questions about product support issues, but can also analyze live support calls for customer sentiment and need for escalation.

- *Customer data monetization.* Many consumer-oriented industries are investigating data monetization in various forms, but
  since this industry has a wealth of data, it has taken the lead
  in monetization. The most common examples are monetizing
  the attention of social media or search users to advertisers,
  or monetizing locations known to mobile telecom providers
  by selling billboards or marketing opportunities for location-
  specific offers. Because this is a sensitive topic to consumers,
  it may be subject to additional regulation in the future.

- *Data center and facility cooling optimization.* Data centers at
  technology firms are major users of electrical energy. Alphabet's DeepMind was the first to develop algorithms that
  could consistently reduce data center cooling energy costs by
  40 percent. Siemens, working with a startup called Vigilent,
  has developed a broader algorithmic approach to optimizing
  facility cooling that is also being used for data centers.[21]

Some of the less common use cases in the industry today—but
which are likely to grow in usage as AI continues to mature—are
the following:

- *Fake media content detection.* Deepfakes, or audio and video
  content that is artificially constructed and not representative
  of reality, are in their early days, but many observers are
  concerned that they will be a major source of disinformation
  in the future. It takes AI to create deepfakes, but AI can
  also identify them. The outcome of this arms race is
  not yet clear, but at least there are potential remedies to
  the problem.

- *Self-healing networks.* Telecom companies live and die by
  the health of their networks, and AI is making it possible to
  predict, restore, and prevent network outages. Just as predictive asset maintenance use cases identify anomalies and

predict failures in a machine, AI applications identify problems and potential issues in networks and resolve them before they occur. At a minimum they let customers know when their services are likely to be restored. Verizon, for example, used AI to predict and prevent two hundred network events in 2017 that could have impacted customers, but many were fixed before they even happened.[22]

- *Language translation services.* Many consumers are now aware of the ability of AI-based smartphone apps to provide basic translation services when traveling to countries or regions with a language other than their own. Similar capabilities are used to translate emails and web pages. Important business documents, however, are usually translated by humans in collaboration with computer-aided translation (CAT) software, which typically presents a proposed translation (in most cases line-by-line) to a human translator, who can accept, reject, or modify the proposed language. CAT tools dramatically accelerate the productivity of human translators.[23]

- *Video content analysis.* Video is being produced at an astounding rate by humans, street security cameras, drones, automobiles, and many other sources. There aren't enough humans available, however, to view and analyze all this content. AI can analyze video for a variety of detection purposes, including motion and/or object, fire or smoke, facial recognition, number recognition, and many more. Paired with natural language generation, it could even tell a story about what it observes.

- *Audio and video mining.* As with video content analysis, content in the form of audio or video can be mined and turned into analyzable structured data. AI can capture many things in such content, including key topics or behaviors, sentiment, and individual humans involved. The AI technologies involved can include natural language processing, computer vision, voice recognition, and deep learning to facilitate each of these objectives.

- *Emotion detection.* Human emotions can be detected with an increasing degree of accuracy through deep learning models. The purposes for doing so range from detecting responses to ads, to identifying road rage in drivers, to noticing fear or anxiety of travelers in airports. However, critics point out that facial recognition is an unreliable guide to human emotions, and other physiological factors may need to be assessed at the same time to improve accuracy.[24]

- *Metaverse creation and management.* Many companies are beginning to pursue the idea of a metaverse—an immersive virtual environment for entertainment, gaming, education, and simulation. AI will play an important role in the metaverse, including automated construction of visual images, video, and language; identity determination; prediction of action and movement; and other components. Meta, the company formerly known as Facebook, has described some of the many roles that AI will play in the metaverse.[25]

AI at the Walt Disney Company

The modern history of AI and analytics at the Walt Disney Company, the $67 billion media and entertainment giant, began in 1995 at the Parks and Resorts business unit. Executives had noticed that airlines had succeeded in improving their margins with yield management, dynamic pricing of airline seats based on supply and demand, and they thought that perhaps the same approach could be applied to hotel room pricing. Mark Shafer, who had worked in revenue management at People Express and Continental Airlines, came to Disney to lead a group originally focused on that use case.

Shafer's hiring led to a dramatic change at Parks and Resorts, and eventually virtually all other Disney business units. His revenue and profit management group now comprises over 250 "cast members," 50 of whom have PhDs. The group is the center of business-focused analytics and AI at Disney, and it has substantially improved the profitability of hotels, parks, Broadway shows, books, and other Disney assets. The group now works across the entire company, and machine learning is one of its primary tools.

Disney's AI is also increasingly visible to customers of its parks. It recently rolled out Genie, an AI-based real-time vacation planning assistant that recommends attractions based on the preferences of a family. The app-based queue management service works in conjunction with the Disney Magic Band, which provides real-time data on where customers are within the parks. The goal is to minimize long lines and to maximize customers' experience.[26]

In its movie business, Disney established a research capability called StudioLAB to explore the use of AI and other technologies to improve movie content. For example, it has improved the usefulness of early test screenings with AI that monitors audience emotions. Disney worked with the California Institute for Technology to place cameras in a movie theater and monitor each face in the audience with deep learning systems. This provides both more data and a more accurate sense of how the audience members are experiencing the movie.[27]

StudioLAB has also created algorithms to review every pixel in a movie frame in order to ensure quality; human analysts only have to look at selected pixels. Other algorithms paint in pixels automatically for a consistent image. The goal is to allow the company's creative storytellers to focus on that activity rather than tedious details.

Throughout these tech-intensive industries, AI is being applied in a variety of use cases. The more aggressive adopters that we have profiled are doing more with AI at an earlier stage than many of their competitors. Our strong expectation is that this emphasis will eventually be reflected in improved operational and financial performance among these already successful organizations.

Note that many of the use cases we've described can be applied across industries. As we've just described, Disney adapted pricing approaches from the airline industry to its entertainment venues. Although the possibilities for use cases across all these industries may be overwhelming for some executives, it's important to consider, and then to adopt, a broad number of them in order to truly transform an organization. Each individual use case can be combined with others in similar areas—customer service, for example—to yield a greater impact. Given the number of possible applications of AI, it's particularly important for senior executives to strategize and prioritize the use cases that are most likely to affect their business and advance their strategies.

CHAPTER 7

Becoming AI Fueled

If you lead or work within a traditional organization, you may be feeling that it is beyond your company's capabilities to become transformed by AI. You may not be a giant retailer like the Kroger Co. or Loblaw with decades of point-of-sale and loyalty data, a giant aircraft manufacturer like Airbus that generates and analyzes massive amounts of sensor data, or a large bank like DBS with a long history of driving its business forward with technology. You may feel that it would be impossible to come up with the talent and resources to go all-in on AI.

But don't despair if you're in this situation. It applies to many companies that for whatever reason have not made extensive use of technology, data, and AI in the past. We are at the beginning of the transformation of companies through AI, and the companies we've described in this book are early adopters.

The good news is that no company was powered by AI a decade ago or so, and for AI-first companies today we can describe several of the paths they took to move in this direction. No superhuman or supernatural traits were required to establish the aggressive adoption of AI. Put simply, the companies saw that they needed much more AI in the future, put people in charge of creating that future, rounded up the needed data, talent, and monetary investments, and moved as rapidly as possible to create new AI capabilities. They all arrived at their destination—or are at least approaching it—through somewhat different paths, but the fundamental steps were the same.

In this chapter we will describe four paths to becoming AI fueled with four examples, including:

- Deloitte, which is transforming itself from an exclusively people-oriented professional services firm to one enabled by smart humans working alongside smart machines;

- CCC Information Solutions, which began as an information provider but has transitioned to an AI-fueled company in the business of facilitating automobile collision repair;

- Capital One, a bank that was an early adopter of analytics and then an early and extensive adopter of AI;

- Well, the only startup we profile in the book, which is creating an AI-based capability to influence health behaviors from scratch.

These are by no means the only options for arriving at an AI-enabled outcome, but they should provide some ideas for any organization interested in taking on the journey.

Deloitte: From a People-Fueled Organization to a People- and AI-Fueled Organization

We're particularly interested in telling Deloitte's story because we work for or with Deloitte—Nitin as the co-head of the AI business for Deloitte US, and Tom as a senior advisor to Deloitte for over a decade. The company is also a great example of a shift in emphasis—

from focusing almost exclusively on using human professionals to perform tasks (beginning in 1845, when Deloitte & Co. was founded in London), to a commitment to being AI fueled and to employing a collaborative mix of humans and machines. Deloitte hasn't fully completed a transition to being AI fueled, and it's hardly abandoning its human workforce; it has almost 350,000 employees worldwide. However, it's well on the way to making extensive use of AI a hallmark of its professional services to clients. That's a big change in emphasis. Jason Girzadas, Deloitte's Managing Principal, Businesses, Global, and Strategic Services, felt strongly that the organization needed to transform itself to play a leading role in a smarter economy, and he is sponsoring the transformation. We've seen in many other cases that becoming AI fueled requires vision, passion, and energy from a senior executive, and Girzadas plays this role, mobilizing the necessary Deloitte stakeholders to support the investment, the mission, and the journey.

AI is one of several priority investments, known as strategic growth opportunities (SGOs), viewed as having an impact on the broad economies in which they operate. Girzadas has overall responsibility for integrating AI (and other priority investment) capabilities into the firm's businesses.

The AI strategic initiative, which is co-headed by Nitin, has a five-year horizon, from 2021 to 2026. The plan specifies how each business can take advantage of AI, and then build a community; create go-to-market relationships with collaborators like Nvidia, Amazon Web Services, and Google; build new practice areas; and invest for the long term. There is a joint focus on enabling internal capabilities and processes with AI, as well as creating new client offerings. Girzadas commented, "Our AI initiative is rooted in a belief that this can transform our cost structure as well as our capability set. It's more of a transformational agenda than an objective to develop 'table stakes' capabilities that everyone in the industry will have. Most leading-edge clients are on this journey, so we have to be at the forefront of addressing new and complex challenges with AI."

Girzadas believes that while Deloitte isn't yet AI-fueled, "We've done what I consider the hardest part—creating mobilization and focus around AI across Deloitte." But there is still, he noted, work to be done in each of the businesses, as well as in infrastructure processes like talent management and finance. The AI initiative also includes capital for substantial acquisitions of AI startups, as well as new service offerings in areas focused on program integrity in government, and assistance to clients in creating and managing smart factories.

This transformation is unusual not only for the magnitude of the change in the business model, but also the way in which it's being adopted. Deloitte, like each of the other "Big 4" global professional services companies, consists of a large network of global member organizations. For the most part, each member firm practices in a single country, and its structures and practices comply with the regulatory environment in that country. Each member firm does business in a similar set of areas, including audit, tax, consulting, and advisory services. Most initiatives at Deloitte take place within member organizations, but the shift toward AI is a global one. Innovation teams in audit, tax, consulting and advisory have been working to create solutions that could be used across the globe—although some may require modifications or configuration to meet local regulations.

There has also been collaboration across business areas—pulling client data together into a common format for analysis can be challenging for both the audit and tax practices, for example, and they've collaborated on tools to do that. Consulting has created a set of AI services and professionals for clients called the AI Foundry, and some of them work with the audit and assurance practice. Upskilling of Deloitte employees in AI methods and tools is a priority for Deloitte, so the AI strategic initiative led to the 2021 creation of the AI Academy, which teaches about AI in the context of client business processes and strategies, and has become a creator of AI talent in the marketplace.

AI in audit and assurance

Deloitte's audit and assurance practice has been working on adding AI capabilities for longer than other Deloitte business units.[1] It started on AI development in 2014 in an innovation and client service delivery group headed by Jon Raphael. The global AI platform, called Omnia, will be used (with local customization) to support the audit business in member firms around the world. It is a set of tools and methods that automates some audit transactions, prioritizes human auditor reviews, and generates insights for clients about their businesses and risks. It will always evolve, but it has already enabled great progress toward having AI perform key tasks in the external audits performed by Deloitte & Touche LLP. From the beginning the practice adopted a best-of-breed approach, including monitoring of new technology startups around the world. Some capabilities were primarily developed internally, while others were largely sourced from external vendors. Kira Systems, for example, is a Canada-based startup with software to extract contract terms from legal documents. This is a very useful capability in the document review process within audits. Auditors have historically had to read through many contracts to extract key terms, but now Kira's natural language processing technology identifies and extracts key provisions in contracts. Omnia functions as a spine for many different internally and externally developed use cases, and new tools can be easily added to it.

Omnia was a global program from the beginning. Although it was first piloted on one US client, it was built with a global mindset. The developers used an agile approach with piloting and quick learning. Omnia development has standardization as a first-order principle, but sometimes local modifications are necessary in particular countries. There are important differences between countries, including data privacy, audit processes and standards, laws and approaches to risk, and business decisioning. Some countries require storage of audit and other types of company data within their boundaries as well. Omnia is also flexible in its ability to support audits for large public clients and small privately held ones.

A key part of auditing a company is getting its key financial and operational data in a format that can be easily analyzed. Companies differ, of course, in their data structures, so extracting the relevant data into an auditing platform can be labor intensive. Deloitte, however, developed the Cortex system to automatically extract journal entries and other needed data from client transactional systems and make it available for analytics. Raphael says that developing a common data model that works across clients was one of the most difficult parts of the Omnia journey, and he somewhat regrets not starting it earlier. Progress was accelerated when the practice hired a chief data officer in 2018.

Omnia's systems have a variety of capabilities. One system, Signal, analyzes publicly available financial data to identify potential risk factors in the client's business. Cortex performs real-time analysis of journal entry datasets to identify patterns relevant to accounting, operations, and controls. Reveal uses predictive analytics to identify areas of audit interest for further scrutiny by human auditors. The most recent addition to the Omnia platform is a trustworthy AI module that evaluates AI models for bias.

Deloitte's audit innovation group follows a common process in developing all its use cases for applying AI to auditing procedures. The five steps in the process are:

1. *Simplify and standardize.* Step one is to create a common, simplified process or procedure for performing the task. At this point, no new technologies are introduced—there is simply the creation of process flows and procedure documentation. A common overall workflow is described, and then individual variations needed for particular jurisdictions are added later.

2. *Digitize and structure.* Digitization—supporting a task with some form of information technology that can collect

data and monitor performance—is a prerequisite to AI technologies that learn from data. Digitization is also the next step in structuring the task. The technology employed typically specifies the order in which activities are performed.

3. *Automate.* Once the task has been digitized and structured, it is usually a straightforward process to automate its performance, typically with some sort of proprietary workflow or even robotic process automation tool. This step reduces the need for manual labor and generally improves cycle time and consistency. For example, Deloitte uses workflow technology to fully automate the confirmation process within an audit, in which letters are sent to multiple external third parties to confirm financial transactions.

4. *Use advanced analytics and analysis.* Automated processes can be monitored with descriptive analytics and may be better tested with predictive or prescriptive analytics. Also, client data is supplemented with external data to further improve the risk assessment process or to identify substantive testing outliers.

5. *Implement cognitive technologies.* The final step in the transformation to an AI-enabled task is to implement AI technologies to make the task more intelligent, thereby learning from auditor interaction with the underlying data (e.g., machine learning). AI tools might learn to perform the task better over time, or they might apply intelligent decisions to an aspect of the task (such as extracting and analyzing contract provisions).

Each of these steps can individually enhance audit quality and provide more timely and meaningful insights for Deloitte auditors and clients.

The process seems to be working. Deloitte's audit innovations won Digital Innovation of the Year at the Digital Accountancy Forum and Awards in the UK in 2022, 2021, 2020, 2018, and 2015. Certainly, other Big 4 firms are embracing AI in audits, but our sense is that Deloitte is in the lead in its pursuit of AI.

The audit innovation group has begun to change its talent model to support AI capabilities as well. It has hired several PhD-level data scientists and data scientist interns, and is increasingly hiring students with educational backgrounds in data and IT.

Raphael says that clients are pleased with the results of the Omnia audits, particularly the level of data-based insights about their business that they reveal. He's confident that AI is improving the quality of audits. The efficiency it enables varies across audits and clients; sometimes it reveals items of interest that require further human auditor investigation, but that improves quality. Omnia has also enabled more work to be done off the client site; it was of tremendous benefit during the Covid-19 pandemic. Raphael is also excited about possibilities for further development of Omnia as well as further global rollout. His group is thinking now about scenarios and simulations that would enable a client to envision alternative climate-related initiatives in their businesses. It's also addressing the possibility of visual displays of journal entries and alternative financial closing simulations. His group is working with Deloitte consultants and their collaborators at Nvidia on complex visual simulations.

AI in tax

Tax is typically bifurcated into forward-looking strategic projects and regulatory compliance activities using historical information. What do both spheres have in common? Complex analysis of large datasets. Historically, that analysis has been performed manually by tax professionals using the best available technology at the time.

Deloitte is pursuing machine learning for tax work, with the idea that combining the efforts of human tax professionals with AI-driven processes can produce a better overall outcome in terms of accuracy, efficiency, and insights.

Beth Mueller, the AI SGO leader for tax of Deloitte's Tax Analytics Insights practice, commented that, "Opportunities for using AI in the tax space abound. We focus on applying highly technical tax law to specific facts. AI-enabled tools and processes will continue to evolve and enable our clients' tax functions to be better business partners in their organizations."

In the area of strategic tax work, tax professionals often make decisions that significantly impact the organization but do so with limited time and information. As the tax department tends to be the last informed about a business transaction, their ability to make the most informed decision can be hindered. However, using artificial intelligence, tax-specific algorithms can be woven into the decision-making process to flag tax considerations earlier and give tax a seat at the table sooner.

A big part of tax compliance, like external audit, is extracting data from a client's transactional systems. Enterprise resource planning (ERP) and other corporate systems are typically not built for tax compliance, so key information must be extracted from them and often recategorized with tax rules in mind. Deloitte has built a platform called Intela to collaborate with clients on engagements, and it includes AI-driven capabilities to extract and categorize data and to deliver insights to tax professionals and clients. One taxation data domain where automatic classification is being applied is the classification of trial balance accounts—providing an initial determination on the tax classification of each account (e.g., deductible vs. nondeductible). Other classifications, such as those involved in indirect tax, are also being automated. Once all the needed data is assembled, Deloitte makes use of robotic process automation and other technology solutions to perform calculations, prepare tax returns, and perform an additional level of quality review checks beyond the human-driven review processes. It can also run the tax data through analytics to identify insights a client may want to consider.

As with audits, tax compliance engagements in the past typically involved significant manual effort for tax professionals— looking up data, taking it from one system and putting it into another, building calculation workpapers, and the like. Much of that manual work has been eliminated, and more will be disappearing over time. This frees up tax professionals to spend more time analyzing the client's tax situation and offering advice on how to improve it. Automating and using AI in corporate tax departments is also consistent with what some global tax authorities have indicated they envision for improving the tax compliance process; at some point, some areas of tax compliance could simply involve one system talking to another, with AI built around it to identify potential accuracy risks.

AI in consulting

Consulting is one of the less structured activities performed by Deloitte professionals, but that doesn't mean there aren't opportunities to apply AI. Nitin leads AI for the consulting practice, and he and his colleagues are pursuing multiple opportunities to change how consultants work using the technology. The opportunities being created broadly fall into two categories: building capabilities and starting new business ventures.

The consulting practice knew that the key to transforming from a people-fueled organization into a people and AI-fueled organization is to rapidly build the necessary capabilities that drive today's smarter economy. Given that AI is increasingly a priority in today's business and society, Deloitte Consulting had to have the requisite AI capabilities to serve its clients. The capabilities included conversational AI, computer vision, using AI techniques to process data from internet of things and edge devices, and the application of AutoML. The aim was to build the necessary knowledge and skill sets in such capabilities at scale; instead of a small, specialized group being able to provide AI services, most Deloitte practitioners could help clients transform their businesses. The contexts for this work included digitizing contact centers, modernizing manufacturing operations to create smart factories, or extending the cloud to the edge of client networks. Within the AI Academy, Deloitte worked with learning institutions to create a customized curriculum for practitioners on the business application of AI and to diffuse the necessary AI capabilities across the consulting practice.

The other area of focus has been to start new business ventures. The aim has been to extend Deloitte Consulting's traditional business to new business models, thus fortifying their market position over the next decade. The AI strategic initiative focuses on the areas in which Consulting already has leading capabilities, and launches new business ventures that will transform the way Deloitte does consulting in those areas in the coming decade.

For example, Deloitte has one of the largest data implementation businesses to help clients migrate their data to the cloud. It is now expanding into how to help clients harness this data and become AI fueled themselves. Deloitte Consulting launched a new business called ReadyAI—an AI capacity as a service—that provides clients with teams with preconfigured complementary skill sets. These teams help clients decide what to do with their data and develop use cases with standard AI processes and tools, including machine and deep learning. ReadyAI enables clients to jump-start their own AI efforts. Unlike a typical consulting engagement, there are no predefined requirements or deliverables, and the teams are often directed by the client.

Another business venture that has been launched involves developing autonomous transactional processes and enabling clients to subscribe to them. Deloitte is historically a leader in implementing

ERP systems. These systems digitize business processes, but the objective of many companies now is to employ autonomous processes where possible. Deloitte, working with its technology vendors, launched a new business using AIOps to automate processes involving multiple transactional systems; these have typically been operated with substantial human labor. Such processes are broken down into discrete transactions, algorithms are built to make intelligent decisions within them, they learn continuously from the data flowing through them, and autonomous actions are triggered. The algorithms are packaged into discrete microservices to which clients can subscribe.

A third business that Deloitte Consulting has launched is to enable smart factories for manufacturing clients. With the ubiquity of sensors on factory floors, massive data is generated at each step in the manufacturing process. Assimilating this data and applying algorithms to analyze and improve processes continuously is what makes a factory smart. Layer in the real-time monitoring and adjustment that could be made with smart cameras, and it yields a system that manufactures, operates largely autonomously, and self-improves. Deloitte is already a leader in implementing global supply chains for organizations, but the smart factory business venture takes it to the next level: an AI-fueled domain at the intersection of manufacturing and supply chain processes.

Deloitte has learned three key lessons from its focus on AI in consulting. To embark on an AI-fueled journey an organization needs to:

- *Modernize what you do today.* Deloitte's focus on building AI capabilities is an initiative to AI-enable and modernize its services so that it advises, implements systems, and operates processes for clients in today's smarter global economy.

- *Build businesses with a long view.* Like most successful organizations, Deloitte recognizes that it needs to build new businesses that will pay dividends over the next decade. The AI strategic initiative involves a multiyear investment plan, dedicated leadership, executive impetus, and a consensus across the organization to strive for long-term benefits as opposed to short-term gain.

· *Explore continuously in a quest for the next.* While the AI strategic initiative is driving a structured program, it is also continuously experimenting with various groups in Consulting to determine the next big idea. An example of this is the quest for autonomous coding of business applications. Many Deloitte Consulting projects involve some form of coding, so the practice is actively experimenting with the use of AI to generate code. The powerful GPT-3 transformer AI program developed by OpenAI proved to be good not only at generating text, but also at generating some types of computer programs. The capability is now at the center of an open-source tool called Codex, which turns English language text descriptions of a program into code. Deloitte consultants are actively investigating under what circumstances Codex can improve productivity and allow nonprogrammers to generate code.

These three lessons have been and will continue to be the guiding principles for the consulting practice's AI initiatives. They drive the AI strategy, investments, and leadership focus. The leaders of the practice also hold the steadfast belief that if Deloitte is going to help its clients become AI fueled, it needs to AI fuel itself as well.

AI in risk and financial advisory

The Risk & Financial Advisory (Advisory) practice at Deloitte focuses on helping clients mitigate risk of various types. In the past it has employed commercially available AI tools to assist with some client projects, such as automatically generating anti–money laundering suspicious activity reports. But with the AI SGO, the practice embarked on a new strategy for AI that is driven by senior principals like Irfan Saif, along with Nitin, the co-head of the AI business for the US firm. These leaders worked to understand the mindset of the executive team, drive change, and create the requisite sense of urgency. The new strategy was based on development of reusable products built by leading data scientists. Ed Bowen, who became head of the practice's AI group in 2020, has a genetics data science background in the pharmaceutical industry, and he quickly accelerated hiring of PhDs and data scientists with backgrounds in math and science.

The Advisory AI group has already developed and delivered four products—two in cybersecurity, one in detecting health-care fraud, and one involving accounting controls. Cybersecurity is an area rich with potential for AI because there is too much data for humans to monitor and understand, and cybercriminals themselves are making increasing use of AI. As in consulting, Advisory has developed a standard AI platform, and has gathered several large-scale data assets. Among all of Deloitte's business units, Advisory's approach to AI is one of the most research oriented and driven by cutting-edge algorithms. If the approach succeeds, the SGO will ensure that it spreads to other business units as well.

In all these different practice areas, there is a clear emphasis on Deloitte professionals working closely with smart machines—augmentation rather than automation. At the moment, humans are still taking on the majority of tasks. At some point in the future, however, there may be a tipping point at which machines perform the majority of tasks for clients, and human beings simply ensure that the machines are doing the jobs they were intended to perform. When virtually all of Deloitte's human employees are collaborating with AI systems, it may be an indication that the future of AI at Deloitte has arrived.

Capital One: From an Analytics-Focused Organization to an AI-Focused One

As we discussed briefly in chapter 6, Capital One has long been known as a data-driven financial services organization. Established in 1994 after spinning off from Signet Bank, the core idea behind the company's formation was information-based strategy—the belief that important operational and financial decisions should be made on the basis of data and analytics. Its founders, Rich Fairbank (who is still CEO) and Nigel Morris, believed that data and analytics could make the company a distinctive, efficient, and profitable credit card issuer. The company used analytics to understand consumer spending patterns, reduce credit risk, and improve customer service. Later, Capital One entered retail and commercial banking, built and acquired a branch network, and entered into various forms of consumer lending. The bank appointed the world's first chief data officer in 2002.[2] Long-time Capital One Chief Information Officer Rob Alexander observed that, "We were creating a better consumer financial services company using data and analytics. We were in many respects the first big data company." When Tom wrote about companies that compete on analytics in 2006, Capital One was one of the few companies featured for building their strategies around data and analytics.[3]

To stay on top, however, organizations need to innovate continually. In 2011, faced with disruption in the banking industry, Capital One made a strategic decision to reinvent and modernize many aspects of its business—from its culture to its operating processes to its core technology infrastructure. "We didn't start on day 1 knowing exactly how this would all unfold over many years," Alexander said. "Our goal was to get to this destination where we were faster and more nimble with new capabilities for customers." The technological aspects of the transformation involved moving to an agile model for delivering software, building a large-scale engineering organization and hiring thousands into digital roles, becoming cloud native and rebuilding apps for the cloud, as well as insisting on modern architectural standards like RESTful APIs, microservices, and building on open-source foundations.

Becoming AI focused

Capital One has also joined the ranks of all-in-on-AI organizations. It originally built up two large machine learning teams, in its credit card line of business and at the enterprise level, but recently combined them into the Center for Machine Learning. There are data scientists building models all across the bank—in cards, risk, customer service, and even staff functions like finance and human resources. Capital One also offers its customers Eno, an intelligent assistant that helps with such tasks as fraud alerts and balance inquiries. The company's executives say that the focus of machine learning and AI is not just on credit decisioning—the classic application for a card issuer—but rather every aspect of customer interaction and operations. As CIO Rob Alexander put it: "Every time we make a decision it's an opportunity to use machine learning—what customers to market to, what products to offer them, what terms accompany the relationship, what rewards to offer, what spending limits to put in place, how to identify fraud, and so forth."

The bank's goal is to provide friction-free experiences that anticipate customer needs, provide the right information and tools before they're needed, and look out for customers and their money. It has applied AI and machine learning to almost every facet of its business, but it is hardly finished with its journey.

Moving to the cloud

How did Capital One modernize its legacy analytics approaches for the world of AI? The primary answer, according to Alexander and his colleagues, was a new generation of technology. Around 2011,

Alexander said, the bank's executives sought to redefine the bank for the future. The cost of key technologies had declined precipitously. The digital channels to which customers were migrating produced substantially more data and the potential for much better customer understanding. The cloud provided the ability to handle data at scale and to integrate disparate data more easily. Alexander and his colleagues concluded that it no longer made sense for the IT organization to build infrastructure solutions. Instead, it should focus on developing great software and business capabilities to serve customers.

Moving data to the cloud was the major outcome of this thinking, and the cloud became a substantial catalyst for Capital One's AI work. The bank started with private clouds in data centers, but then observed what was happening with Amazon Web Services; Alexander felt that his organization could never compete with AWS's scale and resilience. The bank could benefit greatly from the software-driven, massively scalable, instantly provisioned cloud storage and computing capability. Innovative new machine learning tools and platforms were available on AWS and other public clouds. In short, moving to the cloud would enable a new generation of technologies within the bank—not only AI but also mobile and digital customer experiences. By 2020, Capital One had closed its last data center and moved all its applications and data onto the AWS public cloud.[4]

One reason the cloud is so critical is that Capital One is increasingly moving toward a real-time streaming data environment. Mike Eason, a Capital One veteran who is now CIO for Enterprise Data, Machine Learning, and Enterprise Engineering, said that the amount and speed of data is a major difference from the bank's analytics-focused period. He commented in an interview: "The models we used in the 90s were primarily based on batch data—monthly or weekly data, or nightly at best. Now we have a very large amount of streaming data from web and mobile transactions, ATMs, card transactions, and so forth, and we need to analyze it in real time to meet customer needs and prevent fraud. We do still have a data lake to store data, but increasingly we analyze it as it comes in."

Abhijit Bose, who heads the bank's Center for Machine Learning (C4ML), added: "We are becoming a real-time decisioning company. Rich Fairbank talks about it often. We were initially analytics-driven, then we made a transition to data and cloud, and now real-time decisions are the focus. Models analyzing real-time data will drive every function and process in the bank."

The broad emphasis on AI at Capital One is only one component, though one of the most important ones, of a broader transformation journey. Capital One's leaders—starting with its founder, Rich Fairbank—believe that the winners in the economy of the near future will be tech companies with traditional banking capabilities, most importantly risk management. Fairbank had the original vision of a bank that did virtually everything on the basis of data and analytics, and now with massive databases and real-time AI, his vision has been realized and pushed even further. Rob Alexander feels that the bank is in the early stages of a broad transformation toward technology-intensive banking, with AI-based decision-making at its core.

Current AI emphases at Capital One

A key focus at Capital One is employing machine learning at scale throughout the bank. It has ML models in virtually all of its key business processes and is constantly building more and refining those that exist. It's currently focused, for example, on using AI to attack credit fraud, develop personalized rewards offers for customers, and spot ATM scams. It is refining Eno to offer better advice to customers on how to improve their financial lives. It is predicting the activities and needs of customers in online and call center sessions.

Bose, the C4ML leader, has worked at several leading-edge firms in AI. Many data scientists have PhD degrees, but Bose has two—one in engineering mechanics and one in computer science and engineering. He explained in an interview that while some traditional analytics are still employed at Capital One, the goal is to use models that learn from data (i.e., machine learning) as much as possible. ML at scale is a key focus of Bose and the C4ML, using approaches like standard platforms, democratization, libraries for features and algorithms, and large-scale hiring and training.

Capital One is in the process of developing an ML platform that would assist with virtually every aspect of developing, deploying, and maintaining the bank's models over time. (Thousands are already in daily use.) One of its goals is to prevent data scientists from doing the same thing in ten different ways across the bank, which will increase their efficiency, effectiveness, and job satisfaction. The platform helps develop models with various libraries and workflow automation, including feature libraries and automated machine learning tools. Tools in the platform also capture and store model training and execution information, like parameters and outcomes, in a repeatable and searchable way so that models can be audited and reproduced. That information also helps the bank validate and deploy the models. Once in production, models are regularly checked for drift using MLOps tools and methods, and retrained if necessary. In some cases, such as with the Eno intelligent assistant, retraining takes place automatically. In others, there is human oversight through the model regulatory office of the bank.

Even in the area of responsible AI—a major focus of the C4ML— Bose said that the bank would like to build scale and automation into the process when possible. It seeks to maximize explainability, fairness, and ethical considerations by embedding them as objectives within the ML platform. Explainability program libraries and automated bias detection programs will be components of the platform. A few lines of code will call a bias detection library, and its findings will be aggregated and attached to a file sent to a model risk officer.

Capital One is also on a hiring spree for AI talent, hiring thousands of machine learning and related software engineers. In 2021, the bank also developed a 160-hour internal training program for ML engineers previously in other jobs at the bank; Bose said it has received a hugely positive response from employees and is now on its first cohort. C4ML and the human resources function also have recently developed a career job family for the ML engineer role, including career growth, compensation, and advertising for new recruits, joining other job families already in place for data scientists, research scientists, and data engineers. Capital One has incubators or labs at seven US universities and plans to add more to its ecosystem. There may be a future in which faculty members cycle in and out of Capital One for six-month sabbaticals to work on machine learning initiatives.

CIO Alexander asked and answered a key question: "Why hasn't legacy banking been disrupted by tech firms? It probably will be at some point. But we have an opportunity to disrupt our own industry." Indeed, Capital One is hiring some of the best and brightest AI people from those tech companies. Bose came from a senior AI job at Facebook. Rob Pulciani, the executive vice president of AI and Machine Learning Product at the bank, came from Amazon, where he was one of the first executives to lead the Echo/Alexa business. It's clear that Capital One's leaders intend to take a back seat to no one in technology adoption, data management, and machine learning for applications that benefit customers. It's a primary example of a company that once competed on analytics but is now competing on AI.

CCC Intelligent Solutions: From a Data-Focused Organization to an AI-Focused One

A third path to becoming all-in on AI involves a company taking advantage of its extensive data assets and business ecosystem. You may be unaware of an AI-intensive midsize company that is putting advanced technology to work to help automobile insurance companies. But if you've had a car accident requiring substantial work to repair it, you've probably benefitted from their data, their ecosystem, and their AI-based decision-making. CCC was founded in 1980 as Certified Collateral Corporation. The company was originally founded to provide car valuation (collateral) information to insurers to set the value of losses for stolen or damaged vehicles. In 1986 it became CCC Information Services, and in 2021 it became CCC Intelligent Solutions—reflecting its use of AI in its offerings to customers.

Over more than forty years CCC has evolved to collect and manage more and more data, to establish more and more relationships with parties in the automobile insurance economy, and to make more and more decisions with data, analytics, and eventually, AI. For the last twenty-three years, the company has been led by Githesh Ramamurthy, who was previously its chief technology officer. CCC has enjoyed solid growth and is approaching $700 million in annual revenues. This is a midsize company compared to most we have written about in this book, providing an example that companies of many sizes can embrace an aggressive approach to AI in their businesses.

From data to AI

CCC is an example of a company that is building its AI capabilities on top of its extensive data. Its machine learning models are based on over a trillion dollars of historical claims data, billions of historical images, and other data on automobile parts, repair shops, collision injuries, regulations, and multiple other entities. The company also has over 50 billion miles of historical data through telematics and internet of things sensors. It provides data—and increasingly, decisions—to an extensive ecosystem of over 300 insurers, over 26,000 repair facilities, over 3,500 parts suppliers, and all major automobile OEMs. The company's goal is to link these diverse organizations into a seamless network in order to quickly and efficiently process claims. All these transactions take place in the cloud, where

CCC's systems have been based since 2003. They connect 30,000 companies, 500,000 individual users, and $100 billion of commercial transactions through the cloud.

CCC uses AI across many aspects of its business. An investor presentation describes a series of decisions that are made on behalf of its clients that are based—at least in part—on AI. They include:

- Among all available network participants, who needs to be involved in resolving this particular event?

- What local rates and prices apply?

- What local regulations apply?

- Who are the best performing [collision repair] providers in the area?

- What is the exact damage to this specific vehicle and what is needed to restore it?

- What injuries did or did not occur?

- What is the precise cost of resolution?

These decisions are made with some combination of rule-based systems and machine learning. Even the rule-based decisions, however, make use of the company's extensive databases. CCC began developing its first rule-based decisions (called "expert systems" at the time) more than fifteen years ago.

The use of AI takes place at multiple points in the repair process. At its beginning, for example, the process is usually initiated at the first notice of loss (FNOL), when the insurance company first hears of a collision, theft, or damage to the insured vehicle. At that point AI can begin to decide among alternative work steps. Telematics data can be used to accelerate the FNOL without waiting for a customer report. A machine learning model can predict whether the car is likely to be repairable or a total loss—an important and expensive decision for an insurer. CCC's model replaced a checklist on paper, and it was both faster and four to five times more accurate. Later in the process, CCC's AI systems weigh in on which repair facility would be best for the situation, what might be the implications of injuries to the insured driver and passengers, and whether fraud is being committed by parties involved in the process. One insurance company executive told us that the challenge with CCC is finding ways not to turn their entire claims process over to the company.

The long road to image-based estimating

Perhaps the best way to illustrate CCC's transition from a data-oriented business to an AI-oriented one is by relating its journey toward automated—or at least semi-automated—collision repair estimates based on vehicle images. The company had accumulated billions of images over its history, but for most of that time the images were used by human adjusters to assess and record damage. Also, for most of CCC's history, the images were taken by the adjusters at the site of the damaged vehicle, or by repair sites. These photos required professional cameras with special graphics cards to store and send the images.

Almost a decade ago, however, Ramamurthy noticed that amateur cameras were getting better at a rapid pace, and even that they were being incorporated into smartphones. He envisioned a time when the owners of damaged vehicles would be able to take their own photos of their vehicles. He asked his chief scientist at the time to figure out whether this was possible with collision damage images. He engaged several professors at leading universities to help explore the issue. A little later, Ramamurthy began to read about a new AI approach to image analysis—deep learning neural networks—that with enough training data could sometimes equal or exceed human capabilities. It became clear that graphics processing units (GPUs) were very fast at analyzing images, so CCC bought some from Nvidia—the only source at the time. Unlike a traditional CPU, a GPU breaks apart a mathematical problem into smaller problems and solves them in parallel, doing in hours or minutes what would take a CPU days, months, or even years.

Eventually Ramamurthy decided that it was indeed possible that an image analysis solution could be developed. He assembled a pool of talented data scientists, who learned how to map photos onto the structure of different vehicles, and to annotate or label the photos for training the models. CCC had a billion photos and a trillion dollars in claims with which to train. By 2018 the team had some fantastic prototypes running in the company's research lab, but then the challenge became to incorporate the solution into CCC and customer workflows. To have a production system that could be used with every vehicle, every customer, and every type of repair was daunting. The system would also need to incorporate clear thresholds specifying when it should be used and when it shouldn't, as well as guardrails on the AI algorithms.

Shivani Govil, the chief product officer at CCC, discussed how working out all those issues took another three years or so. It also required some fundamental building blocks to be in place for users. For example, she said, "AI driven photo estimating required the adoption of mobile solutions that could capture data and high-resolution pictures from mobile devices." By mid-2021 the system was ready for production deployment. USAA was one of the first customers. In a *Wall Street Journal* article about the adoption of the system, Jim Syring, president of USAA's property and casualty division, commented that, "This is the first time we are using AI-enabled software to process end-to-end auto insurance estimates," and called the new platform its first wholly touchless claims offering.[5]

These capabilities are not intended to replace humans—rather, they are intended to aid users to do even more and focus on the empathetic engagement with customers or on those difficult cases that are the exceptions that cannot be accurately addressed through AI.

Moving forward with data and AI

Data will continue to flow into CCC, and it will be used to improve the predictions of estimating and other models. This will help CCC customers make better decisions, which will be likely to bring CCC more business. This virtuous circle of more data/better models/more business/more data is what makes the ecosystem structure so powerful in combination with AI.

The company continues to grow and invest in its talent pool to take advantage of AI and data science technologies through the claims lifecycle. Govil, a recent hire at CCC, comes from the enterprise software and AI technology domain, and the company is actively recruiting candidates who combine tech leadership with vertical industry depth. Govil elaborates that this is an exciting time to be in the industry, as digital transformation, connected car data, and AI are creating opportunities for growth and new ways of working across the entire insurance ecosystem—one of the key drivers that attracted her to the company.

Better photos and image analysis are not the only technological changes affecting the vehicle insurance industry. Advanced driver assistance systems (ADAS) are already available in many cars and trucks, and autonomous vehicles (AVs) are widely believed to be coming soon. More insurers are moving to pay-as-you-drive insurance based on driver behavior. Once again, CCC is starting with data, and will move eventually toward putting it to work in decision-making. The company has already introduced an offering called CCC VIN Connect that captures both any ADAS equipment that is present on a vehicle in a collision, and the driving behaviors recorded on that vehicle. Ramamurthy said that when autonomous vehicles are available, CCC plans to offer solutions to insurers that would provide insights on who or what was at fault in the accident. Of course, since many of the technical details of AVs are still uncertain, planning for and developing such systems for insurers requires the same types of long-term technology bets that CCC had to make with automated image recognition for collision repairs.

Well: From Scratch to an AI-Fueled Startup

Our last case study isn't starting from something else and moving into AI. Instead, it's a startup that had AI at its core at its inception. Our strong focus in this book has been on legacy companies that have to wrestle with existing technologies, processes, and strategies before they can embrace AI. It is generally much easier for a startup to build up its AI capabilities, so we haven't focused on them. So why describe one at the very end of the book?

There are several reasons for doing so. One is that the experience of an AI startup is an instructive contrast to what legacy companies must go through. Creating substantial change in a large legacy organization can be extremely challenging. Some legacy companies may be tempted to set up independent business units and scale up the approach later after reading about an AI-first startup. They may also acquire startups that have already successfully created AI systems and business processes or models to operate in a new way.

Another reason for discussing this startup is the focus of the company. In earlier chapters we described companies whose primary focus is using AI to change customer behavior, but most of them are not terribly far along in the process. Influencing health behaviors by multiple means is the focus of the startup we'll describe in this chapter. Finally, Gary Loveman, the chairman, CEO and cofounder of this startup, gained a lot of experience with analytics and AI at his previous companies, and he has some interesting thoughts about what's different between the established and startup environments.

The startup company is Well, a behavioral health startup. Loveman was previously a Harvard Business School professor, and then CEO of Harrah's, which became Caesars Entertainment. He was well known in that role as an advocate for the extensive use of analytics in Caesars' business. When he left Caesars, he headed a new business unit at a large health insurer focused on using data, analytics, and AI to change consumer health. Because of the difficulty in modifying existing systems and processes, he found it very difficult to establish the new offerings. For example, he said that just to collect mobile phone numbers and email addresses of the company's members and add them to the company's databases—necessary to provide regular health-based communications—would have cost $30 million in systems changes. Eventually the health insurance company was acquired, the new owner had little interest in the business unit Loveman headed, and he decided to leave and create a startup.

Well is focused on making people healthier, rather than treating them when they get sick. The company is only a bit more than a year old as of this writing, but it has already raised over $60 million from venture capital firms and other investors. Loveman said that most disease management programs from health insurers are focused on the 5 percent of the members who incur 70 percent of the care and costs, but Well serves all members with a broad variety of health conditions. It works with employers, community health organizations, and consumers to engage people in their own health and offer them AI- and human-based advice on how to be healthier.

The company's basic concept is similar to that of Manulife, Ping An, and other large insurers who work with Vitality, the wellness company we described in chapter 5, but the recommendations and behavioral nudges that Well provides are much more personalized. Whereas other companies provide generic exercise and nutrition reminders, Well might recommend specific preventive measures for particular conditions, diagnostic tests, sleep recommendations, or advice about reducing sugar intake. Like other companies in the space, Well also provides rewards, but the rewards are also personalized. Those members who are highly adherent—take their medicines, show up at appointments, and so on—receive lower rewards for good health behaviors. Those who have a low adherence score receive higher rewards.

Data and training for the models

Well uses machine learning to power its personalized recommendations, and of course those models must be trained on data. Well gets its data primarily from insurance claims, although for some members there is also electronic health record data. Claims data is typically three months old, but Well supplements it with members' subjective answers to questions, and the member response to the app. In some cases, Well can garner data from a device like a member's smartwatch. When necessary, Well also asks members to describe aspects of their own health in a brief survey like those a patient might fill out in an emergency care facility.

A recent regulatory change allows consumers to request three years of their insurance claims data, and Well facilitates the process of acquiring the data from insurers. They then ingest it and compare the health situations of members with others of individuals in similar demographics.

Oz Ataman, Well's chief technology officer, told us that the models themselves are a mix of traditional predictive machine learning and causal effects inference for counterfactual predictions under alternative scenarios.[6] Since the company is effectively making recommendations for multiple health interventions over time, it needs to plan a series of clinical content messages—from recommendations to relevant articles to twenty-one-day journeys—that are most likely to yield the desired behavior in the member. This complex set of models also requires a well-defined set of clinical pathways and care intervention journeys for common health conditions.

Well has created a variety of clinical pathways—twenty to thirty of them—in areas like blood pressure, diabetes, behavioral/mental health, hypertension, sleep disorders, and many others. Ataman suggested that the company's AI is less for pattern detection, and primarily for personalization that understands each member's gaps in care (clinical or self), and given those gaps presents clinical content that has the highest likelihood of leading to the desired behavior outcome.

In order to develop and deploy the models, Well needed to hire a talented group of people. A team of data scientists, for example, built the machine learning models. A clinical team consisting of physicians, nurses, and pharmacists developed the clinical pathways and journeys, and this same team aggregates or creates health-care content for members. There is a rewards and incentives team to figure out the rewards that will motivate wellness behaviors. A product team develops the website and mobile user interface. And the majority of the employees are computer engineers who build the applications. The company has about a hundred people in total, based all over the world.

Startup versus legacy

Loveman is in the relatively rare position of leading an AI startup after heading a large public company and a division of another. He found major systems and process change to be challenging at best in his previous roles. But at Well, he said, his team can build new software (AI and otherwise) with the most current modular software. They can easily create application program interfaces (APIs) to any other systems they need to interface with. Being free of a legacy company means being free of legacy technology.

Of course, he said, the CEO role is very different at a startup. He commented:

> At big companies you have staff doing everything—you don't do anything yourself. Now I do almost everything myself. Instead of spending time with governors and senators I spend

a lot of time with my engineers. I am very hands on and involved in the substance of the business, including the technology. I did a lot of research before I launched the company to make sure that the technology and the business model would work. I became convinced that the combination of group support, personalized attention, frequent contact, and incentives could help patients with hypertension, diabetes, weight problems, and other conditions. We're already making it work with several thousand people, but we hope to have a lot more soon.

Ataman, who worked with Loveman at Caesars and at some other large companies, also suggested that most legacy companies' systems were initially built to record transactions. Well's are built from the beginning with the idea of predicting what nudges will lead to desired changes in a member's health behaviors. That's a very different product design, and one that's difficult to accomplish unless it's an organization's primary goal.

Lessons from These AI Journeys

There are important lessons that other organizations can learn from these companies' AI journeys. We'll conclude the book with a description of several of them.

- *Know what you want to accomplish with AI.* Each of these companies has a clear set of ideas about what they want to accomplish in their businesses with AI. For Deloitte, it's to reduce drudgery in the jobs of its professional workers and improve the quality of services. For Capital One, it's to reduce friction and make banking easier for customers. CCC is focused on reducing the administrative burden for automobile insurance companies and their customers when they experience vehicle damage. And Well is using AI to help its customers practice healthy behaviors. All these companies want to use AI to be more financially successful, of course, but that alone is not enough of an objective to identify and develop AI use cases.

- *Start with analytics.* Most of these companies had significant initiatives underway in analytics before moving headlong into AI. Well is an exception, of course, since it's an AI startup, but when Gary Loveman, the CEO, was leading Harrah's and Caesars Entertainment he was a strong advocate of competing on analytics (as Tom wrote about in an earlier book). Each of Deloitte's four business units that we've described had analytics activity underway—both internally and with clients—before moving into AI. Capital One was another excellent example of competing on analytics, as we've described in this chapter. And CCC provided analytics on different aspects of automobile damage and repair from its inception. Of course, AI includes other technologies that are not based on analytics, including autonomous actions, robotics, the metaverse, and others. But any form of machine learning has analytics at its core.

- *Reduce "technical debt" and create a modular, flexible IT architecture.* Gary Loveman's comments about his challenges with legacy IT architectures at his previous employer are sobering. If you want to develop AI use cases and easily deploy them into your IT architecture, you need a flexible, modular infrastructure that communicates largely through APIs—both internal and external to your company. Preparing such an IT architecture even in advance of need can pay off in the long run. If you can't develop such an architecture in a legacy company, you may want to spin off or partner with a startup that doesn't have any technical debt to overcome.

- *Put some data and AI applications in the cloud.* Several organizations described in this chapter (including Capital One and CCC) and elsewhere in the book ascribed much of their success with AI to moving their data into the cloud. Although there are times when premise-based systems may be required for regulatory or systems responsiveness reasons, having data in the cloud often means that it is easier to create AI applications that draw from diverse data sources. Having premise-based data silos will likely mean that your data scientists will spend much of their time attempting to access and integrate data.

- *Think about how to integrate AI with the workflows of your employees and customers.* Inflexible business processes can be as limiting as legacy IT architectures. Each of the companies described in this chapter took pains to integrate AI capabilities with the daily workflows of their employees or customers. Deloitte's simplify and standardize approach in its audit practice is one approach to such process improvements; other companies we described, like Shell, are bringing back the idea of business process reengineering for more radical process change.

- *Marshal some data assets.* Data is typically not a problem for industries such as banking, but the other organizations described in this chapter drove their AI strategies in large part based on the data they could assemble. Integrating data from client transactional systems was perhaps the most challenging component of Deloitte's AI journey. CCC began accumulating data with its first business model and was therefore well prepared for a shift to an AI-based model. Well's business model became feasible when a regulatory change made it possible for customers to get access to their own health insurance claims data.

- *Create an AI governance and leadership structure.* Deloitte's use of the strategic initiative structure for its AI investments and governance provided a helpful overlay on top of its diverse professional services business units. Jason Girzadas provided overall leadership for the effort to integrate AI into its professional services business. Capital One, CCC, and Well all have CEOs with long-term and deep focus on data, analytics, and AI, and have ensured their successful application into strategies and business models.

- *Develop and staff centers of excellence in AI.* Each of the AI-focused companies in this chapter—and all those elsewhere in the book—realized that they needed considerable talent in AI, data engineering, and data science if they were going to be successful in their journeys. Deloitte developed those talent resources for both internal use as well as its consulting clients. Capital One has a large collection of data scientists and machine learning engineers. CCC has an interconnected data science and data engineering team. And Well's data scientists are critical to its ability to develop recommendation and reward models.

- *Be prepared to invest.* AI capabilities are not cheap, and the companies in this chapter have invested heavily in them. Deloitte established a special investment vehicle for AI projects. Capital One is investing heavily in ML platforms, capabilities, and people. CCC went public in 2021 and plans to spend almost a billion dollars investing in its AI and data capabilities for customers. And Well is spending much of the $65 million it has raised on AI and systems capabilities.

- *Work with an ecosystem.* Some of the companies we've discussed, such as CCC, have an ecosystem-based business model. But all the companies work closely with business partners. Deloitte has strong relationships with AI technology collaborators such as Nvidia. Capital One works closely with Amazon Web Services, its cloud partner, and external service vendor organizations. CCC has an incredible ecosystem of insurers, repair shops, parts providers, and other companies. Well works with insurers, community health organizations, and employers. In addition, it is impossible today for a company to succeed with AI without strong relationships with technology partners. And as we've described, some of the most effective AI-based business models are built around ecosystems and platforms.

- *Build solutions across the entire organization.* For small and medium-sized companies, it's taken for granted that AI solutions will work across the entire organization. But for large businesses, this isn't always the case. Deloitte and Capital One, however, illustrate that taking an organization-wide approach can yield considerable benefits. These include sharing solutions across business units and functions, creating a more seamless experience for customers, and providing an opportunity for AI developers to work on diverse types of projects. Organization-wide AI governance structures and centers of excellence will make such a broad approach more feasible.

These lessons from companies pursuing an AI-enabled transformation journey can help any organization move in the same direction. We believe that AI—applied strategically and in large doses—will be critical to the success of almost every business in the future. Data is increasing at a rapid pace, and that's not going to change. AI is a means of making sense of data at scale and of creating smart decisions throughout an organization, and that's not going to change either. AI is here to stay, and the companies that apply it with vigor and intelligence will likely dominate their industries over the next several decades.

NOTES

Introduction

1. For a transcript of Pichai's speech, see *The Singju Post*, May 18, 2017, https://singjupost.com/google-ceo-sundar-pichais-keynote-at-2017-io-conference -full-transcript/.

2. Jack Clark, "Why 2015 Was a Breakthrough Year in Artificial Intelligence," *Bloomberg*, December 8, 2015, https://www.bloomberg.com/news/articles /2015-12-08/why-2015-was-a-breakthrough-year-in-artificial-intelligence.

3. Ash Fontana, *The AI-First Company: How to Compete and Win with Artificial Intelligence* (London: Portfolio, 2021).

4. Thomas H. Davenport, "The Future of Work Now: Intelligent Mortgage Processing at Radius Financial Group," *Forbes*, May 4, 2021, https://www.forbes .com/sites/tomdavenport/2021/05/04/the-future-of-work-now-intelligent-mortgage -processing-at-radius-financial-group/?sh=71bfdec2713a.

5. More details on radius's performance are in Davenport, "The Future of Work Now."

6. Airbus website, https://www.airbus.com/en/innovation/industry-4-0 /artificial-intelligence, accessed December 27, 2021.

7. Ping An Technology website, https://tech.pingan.com/en/, accessed December 27, 2021.

8. See, for example, Thomas H. Davenport, "Competing on Analytics," *Harvard Business Review*, January 2006, https://hbr.org/2006/01/competing-on -analytics, or Thomas H. Davenport and Jeanne Harris, *Competing on Analytics: The New Science of Winning* (Boston: Harvard Business Review Press, 2007; updated and with a new introduction 2017).

9. Deloitte refers to one or more of Deloitte Touche Tohmatsu Limited, a UK private company limited by guarantee ("DTTL"), its network of member firms, and their related entities. DTTL and each of its member firms are legally separate and independent entities. DTTL (also referred to as "Deloitte Global") does not provide services to clients. In the United States, Deloitte refers to one or more of the US member firms of DTTL, their related entities that operate using the "Deloitte" name in the United States, and their respective affiliates. Certain services may not be available to attest clients under the rules and

regulations of public accounting. See www.deloitte.com/about to learn more about their global network of member firms.

Chapter 1

1. Sundar Pichai, "A Personal Google, Just for You," Official Google Blog, October 4, 2016, https://googleblog.blogspot.com/2016/10/a-personal-google-just -for-you.html.

2. Deloitte, "State of AI in the Enterprise" Survey, 3rd edition, 2020, https://www2.deloitte.com/cn/en/pages/about-deloitte/articles/state-of-ai-in-the -enterprise-3rd-edition.html.

3. Unless otherwise cited, all statements and quotes come from interviews conducted by the authors.

4. IBM Watson Global AI Adoption Index 2021, https://filecache.mediaroom .com/mr5mr_ibmnews/190846/IBM's%20Global%20AI%20Adoption%20Index %202021_Executive-Summary.pdf.

5. Sam Ransbotham et al., "Winning with AI: Findings from the 2019 Artificial Intelligence Global Executive Study and Research Report," *MIT Sloan Management Review*, October 15, 2019, https://sloanreview.mit.edu/projects /winning-with-ai/.

6. Deloitte, "State of AI in the Enterprise" Survey, 2nd edition, 2018, https://www2.deloitte.com/us/en/insights/focus/cognitive-technologies/state -of-ai-and-intelligent-automation-in-business-survey-2018.html.

7. Thomas H. Davenport and Randy Bean, "Companies Are Making Serious Money with AI," *MIT Sloan Management Review*, February 17, 2022, https:// sloanreview.mit.edu/article/companies-are-making-serious-money-with-ai/.

8. Thomas H. Davenport and Julia Kirby, *Only Humans Need Apply: Winners and Losers in the Age of Smart Machines* (New York: Harper Business, 2016); also Thomas H. Davenport and Steven Miller, *Working with AI: Real Stories of Human-Machine Collaboration* (Cambridge, MA: MIT Press, 2022).

9. Thomas H. Davenport, "Continuous Improvement and Automation at Voya Financial," *Forbes*, December 9, 2019, https://www.forbes.com/sites /tomdavenport/2019/12/09/continuous-improvement-and-automation-at-voya -financial/?sh=4f8441ac46a4.

10. Deloitte, "State of AI in the Enterprise" Survey.

11. Veronica Combs, "Guardrail Failure: Companies Are Losing Revenue and Customers Due to AI Bias," *TechRepublic*, January 11, 2022, https://www .techrepublic.com/article/guardrail-failure-companies-are-losing-revenue-and -customers-due-to-ai-bias/.

12. Reid Blackman, "If Your Company Uses AI, It Needs an Institutional Review Board," *Harvard Business Review*, April 1, 2021.

13. John Hagel and John Seely Brown, "Great Businesses Scale Their Learning, Not Just Their Operations," *Harvard Business Review*, June 7, 2017,

https://hbr.org/2017/06/great-businesses-scale-their-learning-not-just-their
-operations.

14. Zheng Yiran, "AI Strikes Note of Confidence in Arts," *China Daily,*
September 23, 2019, https://global.chinadaily.com.cn/a/201909/23/WS5d882
a3da310cf3e3556ce14.html.

Chapter 2

1. Randy Bean and Thomas H. Davenport, "Companies Are Failing in
Their Efforts to Become Data-Driven," *Harvard Business Review,* February 5,
2019, https://hbr.org/2019/02/companies-are-failing-in-their-efforts-to-become
-data-driven.

2. Joanna Pachner, "Choice President: Why Sarah Davis Is the Leader
Loblaw Needs Right Now," *The Globe and Mail,* January 28, 2020, https://www
.theglobeandmail.com/business/rob-magazine/article-choice-president-why
-sarah-davis-is-the-leader-loblaw-needs-right-now/.

3. Deloitte Insights, "2021 State of AI in the Enterprise," Survey Report,
4th Edition, https://www2.deloitte.com/content/dam/insights/articles/US144384
_CIR-State-of-AI-4th-edition/DI_CIR-State-of-AI-4th-edition.pdf.

4. Thomas H. Davenport and Ren Zhang, "Achieving Return on AI Projects," *MIT Sloan Management Review,* July 20, 2021, https://sloanreview.mit
.edu/article/achieving-return-on-ai-projects/.

5. Deloitte Insights, "2021 State of AI in the Enterprise."

6. This section draws from Thomas H. Davenport and George Westerman,
"How HR Leaders Are Preparing for the AI-Enabled Workforce," *MIT Sloan
Management Review,* March 17, 2021, https://sloanreview.mit.edu/article/how
-hr-leaders-are-preparing-for-the-ai-enabled-workforce/.

7. J. Loucks, T. Davenport, and D. Schatsky, "State of AI in the Enterprise,
2nd Edition: Early Adopters Combine Bullish Enthusiasm with Strategic Investments," PDF file (New York: Deloitte Insights, 2018), https://www2.deloitte.com.

8. T. Cullen, "Amazon Plans to Spend $700 Million to Retrain a Third of
Its US Workforce in New Skills," CNBC, July 11, 2019, https://www.cnbc.com
/2019/07/11/amazon-plans-to-spend-700-million-to-retrain-a-third-of-its-work
force-in-new-skills-wsj.html.

9. Wei-Shen Wong, "DBS Bank Grows Its Team of Data Translators,"
Waters Technology, July 29, 2019, https://www.waterstechnology.com/data
-management/4456596/dbs-bank-grows-its-team-of-data-translators.

10. "JPMorgan Chase Makes $350 Million Global Investment in the Future
of Work," JPMorgan Chase press release, March 18, 2019, https://www
.jpmorganchase.com/news-stories/jpmorgan-chase-global-investment-in-the
-future-of-work.

11. Erik Brynjolfsson, Tom Mitchell, and Daniel Rock, "What Can Machines
Learn, and What Does It Mean for Occupations and the Economy?" *AEA Papers*

and Proceedings, May 2018, pp. 43–47, https://www.aeaweb.org/articles?id=10
.1257/pandp.20181019.

12. Davenport and Westerman, "How HR Leaders Are Preparing for the AI-
Enabled Workforce."

13. Thomas H. Davenport, "Building a Culture that Embraces Data and AI,"
Harvard Business Review, October 28, 2019, https://hbr.org/2019/10/building-a
-culture-that-embraces-data-and-ai.

Chapter 3

Epigraph: Taken from Alex Connock and Andrew Stephen, "We Invited an AI
to Debate Its Own Ethics in the Oxford Union—What It Said Was Startling,"
The Conversation, December 10, 2021, https://theconversation.com/we-invited
-an-ai-to-debate-its-own-ethics-in-the-oxford-union-what-it-said-was-startling
-173607.

1. Sam Ransbotham et al., "The Cultural Benefits of Artificial Intelligence
in the Enterprise," *MIT Sloan Management Review Report*, November 2, 2021,
https://sloanreview.mit.edu/projects/the-cultural-benefits-of-artificial-intelli
gence-in-the-enterprise/.

2. Steven LeVine, "Our Economy Was Just Blasted Years into the Future,"
Medium website, May 25, 2020, https://marker.medium.com/our-economy-was
-just-blasted-years-into-the-future-a591fbba2298.

3. Roberto Baldwin, "Self-Driving Cars Are Taking Longer to Build than
Everyone Thought," *Car and Driver*, May 10, 2020, https://www.caranddriver
.com/features/a32266303/self-driving-cars-are-taking-longer-to-build-than
-everyone-thought/.

4. Thomas H. Davenport, "Getting Real about Autonomous Cars," MIT
Initiative on the Digital Economy blog post, April 3, 2017, https://ide.mit.edu
/insights/getting-real-about-autonomous-cars/.

5. Job description for "Research Scientist, Machine-Assisted Cognition,"
Toyota Research Institute, https://www.simplyhired.com/search?q=toyota
+research+institute&job=IKITbaYj1djMYyHDHXyGr-9sbM2sxZvZ5eCw4DFFo
2fIRUkQGllRXw, accessed August 2, 2021.

6. "Toyota Research Institute Bets Big in Vegas on 'Toyota Guardian'
Autonomy," Toyota press release, January 7, 2019, https://pressroom
.toyota.com/toyota-research-institute-bets-big-in-vegas-on-toyota-guardian
-autonomy/.

7. James Burton, "The World's Top-10 Wealth Management Firms by
AUM," Wealth Professional website, May 5, 2021, https://www.wealthprofessi
onal.ca/news/industry-news/the-worlds-top-10-wealth-management-firms-by
-aum/355658.

8. See, for example, https://www.forbes.com/sites/barrylibert/2019/10/29
/platform-models-are-coming-to-all-industries/?sh=4ccb418962e7.

9. For a more detailed discussion of ecosystems, see Arnoud De Meyer and Peter Williamson, *The Ecosystem Edge* (Palo Alto, CA: Stanford Business Books, 2020).

10. C3.ai, "Shell, C3.ai, Baker Hughes, and Microsoft Launch the Open AI Energy Initiative, an Ecosystem of AI Solutions to Help Transform the Energy Industry," C3.AI press release, February 1, 2021, https://c3.ai/shell-c3-ai-baker -hughes-and-microsoft-launch-the-open-ai-energy-initiative-an-ecosystem-of-ai -solutions-to-help-transform-the-energy-industry/.

11. Dan Jeavons and Christophe Vaessens, "Q&A: What Does Open AI Mean for Energy Production?" Shell website, March 24, 2021, https://www.shell .com/business-customers/catalysts-technologies/resources-library/ai-in-energy -sector.html.

12. Diabetes Prevention Program Research Group, "Reduction in the Incidence of Type 2 Diabetes with Lifestyle Intervention or Metformin," *New England Journal of Medicine* 346, no. 6 (February 7, 2002), https://www.nejm .org/doi/10.1056/NEJMoa012512.

13. "Kroger Using Data, Technology to 'Restock' for the Future," *Consumer Goods Technology*, October 17, 2017, https://consumergoods.com/kroger-using -data-technology-restock-future.

14. Kroger Investor Conference, October 11, 2017, https://s1.q4cdn.com /137099145/files/doc_events/2017/10/1/Presentation.pdf.

15. Russell Redman, "Kroger to 'Lead with Fresh, Accelerate with Digital," *Supermarket News*, April 1, 2021, https://www.supermarketnews.com/retail -financial/kroger-lead-fresh-accelerate-digital-2021.

16. Ocado Group website, "About Us: What We Do, How We Use AI," https:// www.ocadogroup.com/about-us/what-we-do/how-we-use-ai, accessed December 26, 2021.

17. See, for example, Sinan Aral, *The Hype Machine: How Social Media Disrupts Our Elections, Our Economy, and Our Health—and How We Must Adapt* (New York: Crown, 2021).

18. Progressive Insurance, "Telematics Devices for Car insurance," Progressive website, https://www.progressive.com/answers/telematics-devices-car -insurance/, accessed March 24, 2022.

Chapter 4

1. Thomas H. Davenport, Theodoros Evgeniou, and Thomas C. Redman, "Your Data Supply Chains Are Probably a Mess," *Harvard Business Review*, June 24, 2021, https://hbr.org/2021/06/data-management-is-a-supply-chain -problem.

2. Katherine Noyes, "AI Can Ease GDPR Burden," Deloitte Insights for CMOs, *Wall Street Journal*, June 4, 2018, https://deloitte.wsj.com/articles/ai-can -ease-gdpr-burden-1528084935.

Chapter 5

1. Anthem Corporate and Social Responsibility Report, "Becoming a Digital-First Platform for Health," 2020, https://www.antheminc.com/annual-report/2020/becoming-a-digital-first-platform-for-health.html.

2. See, for example, Thomas H. Davenport, "The Future of Work Now: Ethical AI at Salesforce," *Forbes,* May 27, 2021, https://www.forbes.com/sites/tomdavenport/2021/05/27/the-future-of-work-now-ethical-ai-at-salesforce/?sh=16195cd53eb6.

3. Margaret Mitchell et al., "Model Cards for Model Reporting," paper presented at FAT*'19: Conference on Fairness, Accountability, and Transparency, January 2019, arXiv:1810.03993.

4. Isabel Kloumann and Jonathan Tannen, "How We're Using Fairness Flow to Help Build AI That Works Better for Everyone," Facebook blog post, March 31, 2021, https://ai.facebook.com/blog/how-were-using-fairness-flow-to-help-build-ai-that-works-better-for-everyone/.

5. Shirin Ghaffary, "Google Says It's Committed to Ethical AI Research. Its Ethical AI Team Isn't So Sure," *Vox,* June 2, 2021, https://www.vox.com/recode/22465301/google-ethical-ai-timnit-gebru-research-alex-hanna-jeff-dean-marian-croak.

6. Paresh Dave and Jeffrey Dastin, "Money, Mimicry and Mind Control: Big Tech Slams Ethics Brakes on AI," Reuters, September 8, 2021, https://www.reuters.com/technology/money-mimicry-mind-control-big-tech-slams-ethics-brakes-ai-2021-09-08/.

7. Ping An Group, "AI Ethical Governance Statement and Policies of Ping An Group," https://group.pingan.com/resource/pingan/ESG/Sustainable-Business-Integration/ping-an-group-ai-ethics-governance-policy.pdf, accessed December 21, 2021.

8. Partnership on AI, home webpage, https://partnershiponai.org/, accessed March 24, 2022.

9. EqualAI, "Checklist for Identifying Bias in AI," https://www.equalai.org/assets/docs/EqualAI_Checklist_for_Identifying_Bias_in_AI.pdf, accessed December 21, 2021.

Chapter 6

1. Deloitte AI Institute, "The AI Dossier," 2021, https://www2.deloitte.com/us/en/pages/consulting/articles/ai-dossier.html.

2. Alamira Jouman Hajjar, "Retail Chatbots: Top 12 Use Cases & Examples in 2022," AIMultiple website, February 11, 2022, https://research.aimultiple.com/chatbot-in-retail/.

3. Cecelia Kang, "Here Comes the Full Amazonification of Whole Foods," *The New York Times,* February 28, 2022, https://www.nytimes.com/2022/02/28/technology/whole-foods-amazon-automation.html.

4. Judson Althoff, "Orsted Uses AI and Advanced Analytics to Help Power a Greener Future," LinkedIn, March 3, 2021, https://www.linkedin.com/pulse /%C3%B8rsted-uses-ai-advanced-analytics-help-power-greener-future-althoff.

5. This use case is described in Thomas H. Davenport, "Pushing the Frontiers of Manufacturing AI at Seagate," *Forbes*, January 27, 2021, https:// www.forbes.com/sites/tomdavenport/2021/01/27/pushing-the-frontiers-of -manufacturing-ai-at-seagate/?sh=3d1e524cc4f.

6. Nitin Aggarwal and Rostam Dinyari, "Seagate and Google Predict Hard Disk Drive Failures with ML," Google Cloud Blog, May 7, 2021, https://cloud .google.com/blog/products/ai-machine-learning/seagate-and-google-predict-hard -disk-drive-failures-with-ml.

7. The Haven Life use case is described in Thomas H. Davenport, "The Future of Work Is Now: The Digital Life Underwriter," *Forbes*, October 28, 2019, https://www.forbes.com/sites/tomdavenport/2019/10/28/the-future-of -work-is-nowdigital-life-underwriter-at-haven-life/?sh=4fc2332d6b54.

8. Steven Miller and Thomas H. Davenport, "A Smarter Way to Manage Mass Transit in a Smart City: Rail Network Management at Singapore's Land Transport Authority," AI Singapore website, May 27, 2021, https://aisingapore .org/2021/05/a-smarter-way-to-manage-mass-transit-in-a-smart-city-rail-network -management-at-singapores-land-transport-authority/.

9. Karen Hao, "AI Is Sending People to Jail—and Getting It Wrong," *MIT Technology Review*, January 21, 2019, https://www.technologyreview.com/2019 /01/21/137783/algorithms-criminal-justice-ai/.

10. Thomas H. Davenport and Rajeev Ronanki, "Artificial Intelligence for the Real World," *Harvard Business Review*, January-February 2018, pp. 108– 116, https://hbr.org/2018/01/artificial-intelligence-for-the-real-world.

11. National Oceanic and Atmospheric Administration, "NOAA Artificial Intelligence Strategy: Analytics for Next Generation Earth Science," February 2020, https://nrc.noaa.gov/LinkClick.aspx?fileticket=0I2p2-Gu3rA%3d &tabid= 91&portalid=0.

12. David F. Engstrom, Daniel E. Ho, Catherine M. Sharkey, and Mariano-Florentino Cuéllar, "Government by Algorithm: Artificial Intelligence in Federal Administrative Agencies," report to the Administrative Conference of the United States, February 2020, pp. 38–39, https://www-cdn.law.stanford.edu/wp -content/uploads/2020/02/ACUS-AI-Report.pdf.

13. See U.S. Department of Veterans Affairs, Office of Research and Development, "National Artificial Intelligence Institute (NAII)," https://www.research .va.gov/naii/.

14. Kate Conger, "Justice Department Drops $2 Million to Research Crime-Fighting AI," Gizmodo, February 27, 2018; and DOJ's solicitation for the program can be found at https://nij.gov/funding/Documents/solicitations/NIJ-2018-14000.pdf.

15. Tony Kingham, "US S&T's Transportation Security Laboratory Evaluates Artificial Intelligence and Machine Learning Technologies," Border Security

Report, September 11, 2020, https://border-security-report.com/us-sts
-transportation-security-laboratory-evaluates-artificial-intelligence-and
-machine-learning-technologies/.

16. Richard Rubin, "AI Comes to the Tax Code," *The Wall Street Journal*,
February 6, 2020, https://www.wsj.com/articles/ai-comes-to-the-tax-code
-11582713000.

17. John Keller, "Pentagon to Spend $874 Million on Artificial Intelligence
(AI) and Machine Learning Technologies Next Year," *Military and Aerospace
Electronics*, June 4, 2021, https://www.militaryaerospace.com/computers/article
/14204595/artificial-intelligence-ai-dod-budget-machine-learning.

18. Singapore National Research Foundation, AI Singapore website, accessed
June 15, 2022, https://nrf.gov.sg/programmes/artificial-intelligence-r-d
-programme.

19. Singapore Monetary Authority, "Veritas Initiative Addresses Implementation Challenges in the Responsible Use of Artificial Intelligence and Data
Analytics," press release, January 6, 2021, https://www.mas.gov.sg/news/media
-releases/2021/veritas-initiative-addresses-implementation-challenges.

20. Alex Woodie, "Inside Cisco's Machine Learning Model Factory," Datan-
ami, January 12, 2015, https://www.datanami.com/2015/01/12/inside-ciscos
-machine-learning-model-factory/.

21. Max Smolaks, "AI for Data Center Cooling: More Than a Pipe Dream,"
Data Center Dynamics website, April 12, 2021, https://www.datacenterdynamics
.com/en/analysis/ai-for-data-center-cooling-more-than-a-pipe-dream/.

22. Bernard Marr, "The Amazing Ways Verizon Uses AI and Machine
Learning to Improve Performance," *Forbes*, June 22, 2018, https://www.forbes
.com/sites/bernardmarr/2018/06/22/the-amazing-ways-verizon-uses-ai-and
-machine-learning-to-improve-performance/?sh=1478c22f7638.

23. See, for example, Thomas H. Davenport, "The Future of Work Now: The
Computer-Assisted Translator and Lilt," *Forbes*, June 29, 2020, https://www
.forbes.com/sites/tomdavenport/2020/06/29/the-future-of-work-now-the
-computer-assisted-translator-and-lilt/?sh=19fb4bc73890.

24. See, for example, Douglas Heaven, "Why Faces Don't Always Tell the
Truth about Feelings," *Nature*, February 26, 2020, https://www.nature.com
/articles/d41586-020-00507-5.

25. Kolawole Samuel Adebayo, "Meta Describes How AI Will Unlock the
Metaverse," VentureBeat website, March 2, 2022, https://venturebeat.com/2022
/03/02/meta-describes-how-ai-will-unlock-the-metaverse/.

26. Sarah Whitten, "Disney Launches Genie, an All-In-One App for Park
Visitors to Plan Trips and Skip Long Lines," CNBC website, August 18, 2021,
https://www.cnbc.com/2021/08/18/disneys-genie-app-is-an-all-in-one-trip
-planner-for-its-theme-parks.html.

27. Robert Perkins, "Neural Networks Model Audience Reactions to Movies,"
California Institute of Technology, July 21, 2017, https://www.caltech.edu/about
/news/neural-networks-model-audience-reactions-movies-79098.

Chapter 7

1. Thomas H. Davenport, "The Power of Advanced Audit Analytics," Deloitte report, 2016, https://www2.deloitte.com/content/dam/Deloitte/us /Documents/deloitte-analytics/us-da-advanced-audit-analytics.pdf.

2. Among many other sources, see the "Early CDO Appointments" in the Wikipedia entry for Chief Data Officers: https://en.wikipedia.org/wiki/Chief _data_officer#Early_CDO_appointments.

3. Thomas H. Davenport, "Competing on Analytics," *Harvard Business Review*, January 2006, https://hbr.org/2006/01/competing-on-analytics.

4. Derek du Preez, "Capital One Closes All Its Data Centres and Goes All In with AWS," *Diginomica,* January 12, 2021, https://diginomica.com/capital -one-closes-its-data-centres-and-goes-all-aws.

5. Angus Loten, "AI Helps Auto Insurers Cost Out Collisions in Seconds," *The Wall Street Journal*, November 2, 2021, https://www.wsj.com/articles/ai -helps-auto-insurers-cost-out-collisions-in-seconds-11635866345.

6. For a discussion of such models, see Mattia Prosperi et al., "Causal Inference and Counterfactual Prediction in Machine Learning for Actionable Healthcare," *Nature Machine Intelligence* 2 (2020): 369–375, https://doi.org/10 .1038/s42256-020-0197-y.

INDEX

Page numbers ending in *f* refer to figures, and those ending in *t* refer to tables.

ACKNOWLEDGMENTS

We couldn't have written this book if a good number of intrepid executives hadn't made their companies leaders in the application of AI to their businesses, and then been willing to talk with us about their successes and struggles. So, in alphabetical order of their organizations, we'd like to thank Fabrice Valentin and Romaric Redon at Airbus; Rajeev Ronanki, Ashok Chennuru, and Shawn Wang at Anthem; Caroline Uhler and Anthony Philippakis at the Broad Institute; Githesh Ramamurthy, Shivani Govil, and Marc Fredman at CCC Intelligent Solutions; Chris Donovan at Cleveland Clinic; Piyush Gupta and Sameer Gupta at DBS Bank; Jason Girzadas, Jon Raphael, Ed Bowen, Irfan Saif, Juan Tello, Beth Mueller, and Adoni Kalatzis at Deloitte (as a case example within the book); Vipin Gopal at Eli Lilly; Milen Mahadevan and several of his colleagues at Kroger/ 84.51°; Jodie Wallis at Manulife; Jeff McMillan at Morgan Stanley; Jing Xiao at Ping An; Keith Polaski at radius financial group; Phil Thomas, Grace Lee, and Peter Serenita at Scotiabank; Dan Jeavons at Shell; Andy Hill and Giles Pavey at Unilever; and Gary Loveman and Ozgun Ataman at Well. All of them were generous with their time and ideas.

A Deloitte team, including Debbra Stolarik, Kim Cordes, Jennifer O'Neill, Melissa Neumann, Jamie Palmeroni-Lavis, Christina Scoby, Jeremy Covert, and Charley Chen, helped with every step of the book. A special thanks to Kate Schmidt and Sanjana Jain, who leaned in to keep us on track and managed timelines, relationships, complexities, and approvals to make this book a success; and Sandie

Witas, who kept up with Nitin's schedule. Without them, the book would probably roll off the presses in 2026. And finally, thank you to Beena Ammanath, who suggested we write this book from the onset.

For general support, comfort, and love—and for putting up with him for four decades—Tom thanks his wife, Jodi. He is also grateful for his dog, Pancho, who lay at his feet while Tom wrote much of the book. Nitin thanks Jason Girzadas for his leadership, Andrew Vaz for his inspiration, Dave Couture for his guidance, Irfan Saif for his partnership, Jack Russi for his friendship, Amy Feirn for her mentorship, Ambar Chowdhury for his vision, Matt David for his steadfastness, Nishita Henry for her pioneering spirit, Costi Perricos for his passion in AI, and Joe Ucuzoglu for his belief in the journey. On a personal note, Nitin thanks his wife, Fang, for inspiring him to be an author and narrating his experiences and observations for the benefit of society at large. And for his son, Adrian, Nitin hopes this book will motivate him to achieve his own aspirations in the years to come.

ABOUT THE AUTHORS

Thomas H. Davenport is the President's Distinguished Professor of IT and Management at Babson College, a visiting professor at Oxford University's Saïd Business School, a fellow of the MIT Initiative on the Digital Economy, and a senior advisor to Deloitte's AI practice. He has published over twenty books and over 300 articles for *Harvard Business Review*, *MIT Sloan Management Review*, and many other publications. He writes columns for *Forbes*, *MIT Sloan Management Review*, and the *Wall Street Journal*. He has been named one of the world's top 25 consultants by *Consulting* magazine, one of the 100 most influential people in the IT industry by Ziff-Davis magazines, and one of the world's top 50 business school professors by *Fortune* magazine. He's also been a LinkedIn Top Voice for both the education and tech sectors.

Nitin Mittal is a principal with Deloitte Consulting LLP. He currently serves as the US Artificial Intelligence (AI) Strategic Growth Offering Leader. He was the 2019 recipient of the AI Innovator of the Year award at the AI Summit, New York. He specializes in advising clients to achieve competitive advantage through data and AI-powered transformations that promote amplified intelligence and enable our clients to make strategic choices and transform ahead of disruption.

Throughout his career, Nitin has served as a trusted advisor on data, analytics, and AI and has worked across a number of industry sectors. His primary focus has been working with life sciences and health care clients, implementing large-scale data programs that promote organizational intelligence, and using advanced analytics and AI to drive insights and business strategy.